I've decided to enter this material, glass, from a backdoor—the hot-shop dumpsters.

Picking the residue from the glass-blowing process, the discarded shatters are rationalized through other beings: a misty inspiration, an esoteric joke, the MacGuffin, archeological research, a pedantic excuse, or the others. So let me, this skillful amateur, a genuine liar, escort you into this field of glass.

于是我决定，从一个秘密的门——工作室的垃圾桶——来进入这种材料：玻璃。

　　作为玻璃工艺制作过程中产生的残渣，这些碎片被我精心挑选并通过别的存在方式赋予价值。比如说游离的灵感，限于圈内人的笑话，希区考克的麦高芬，类似于考古的研究，卖弄学问的借口……或者其他。然则，请允许我这位资深业余家，一个真诚的骗子，带你走进玻璃之地。

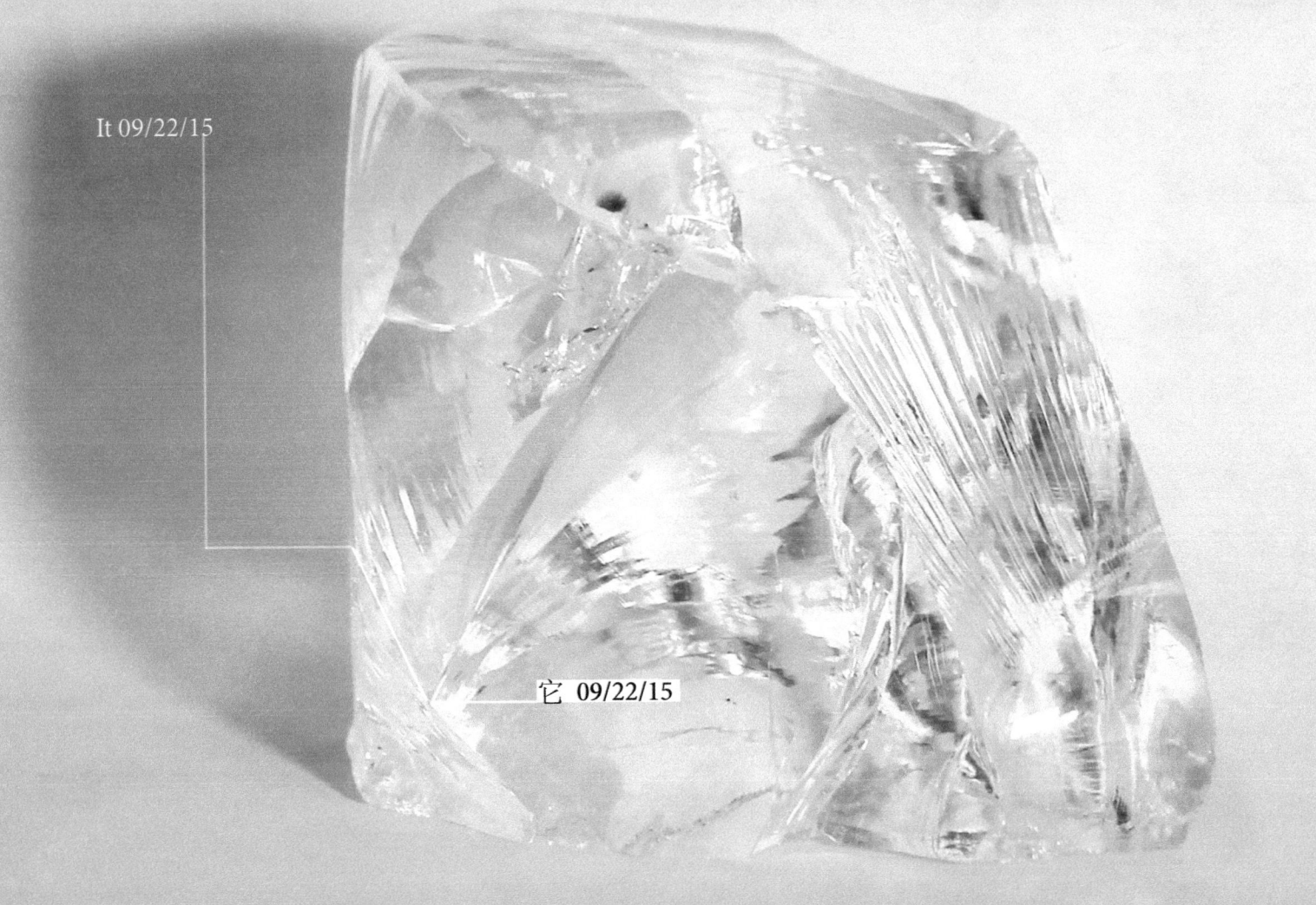

It 09/22/15

它 09/22/15

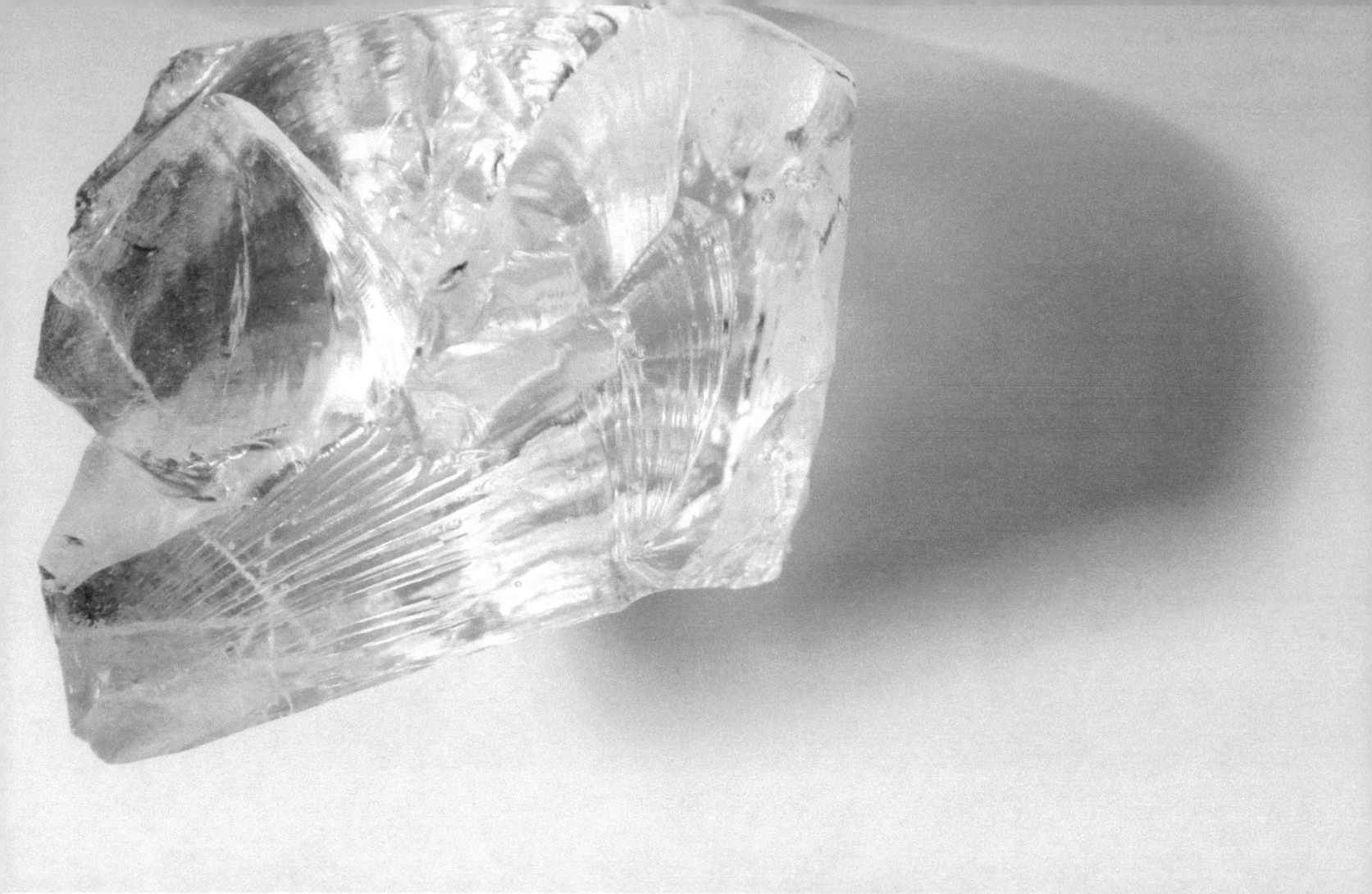

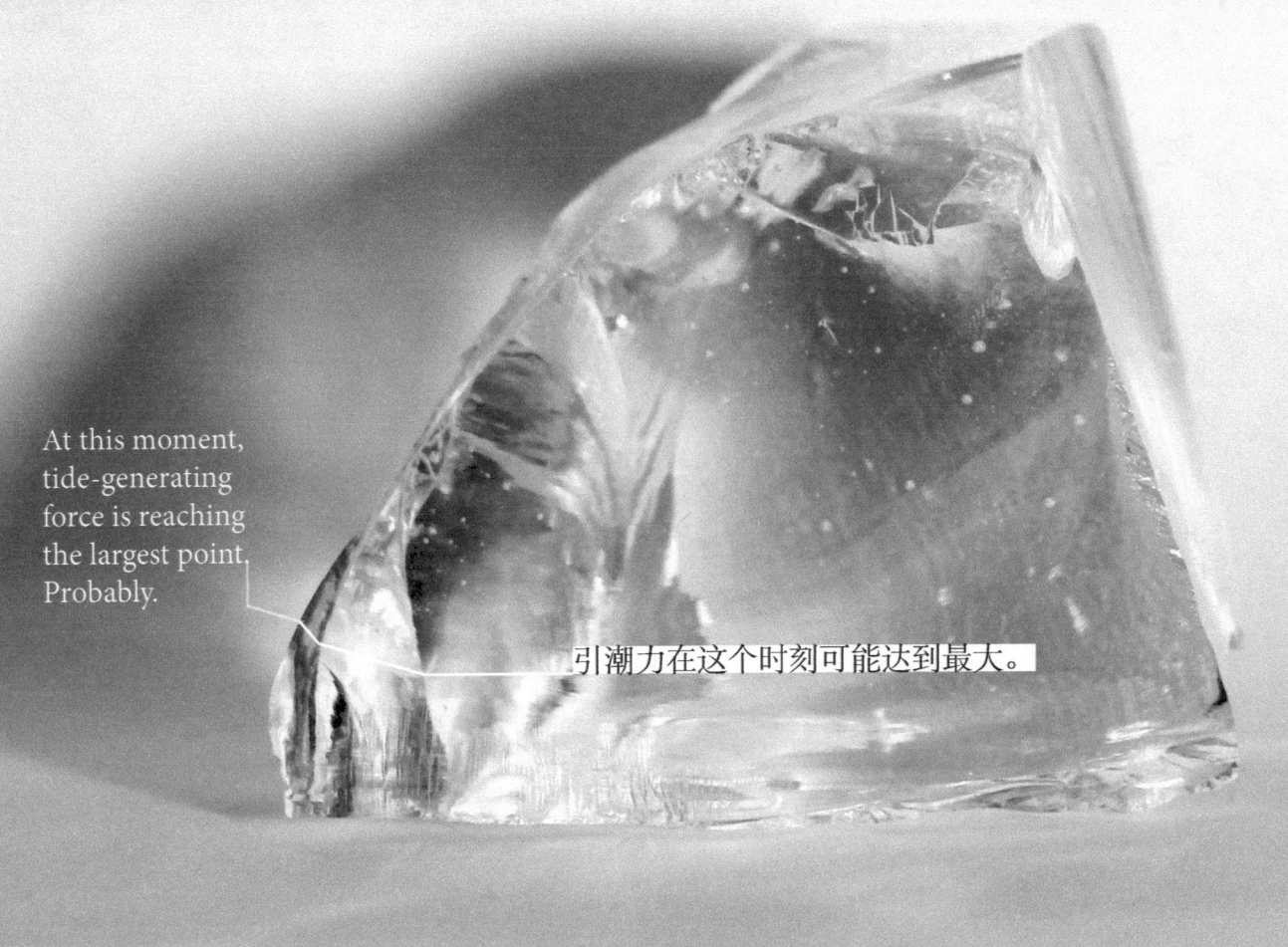

At this moment,
tide-generating
force is reaching
the largest point.
Probably.

引潮力在这个时刻可能达到最大。

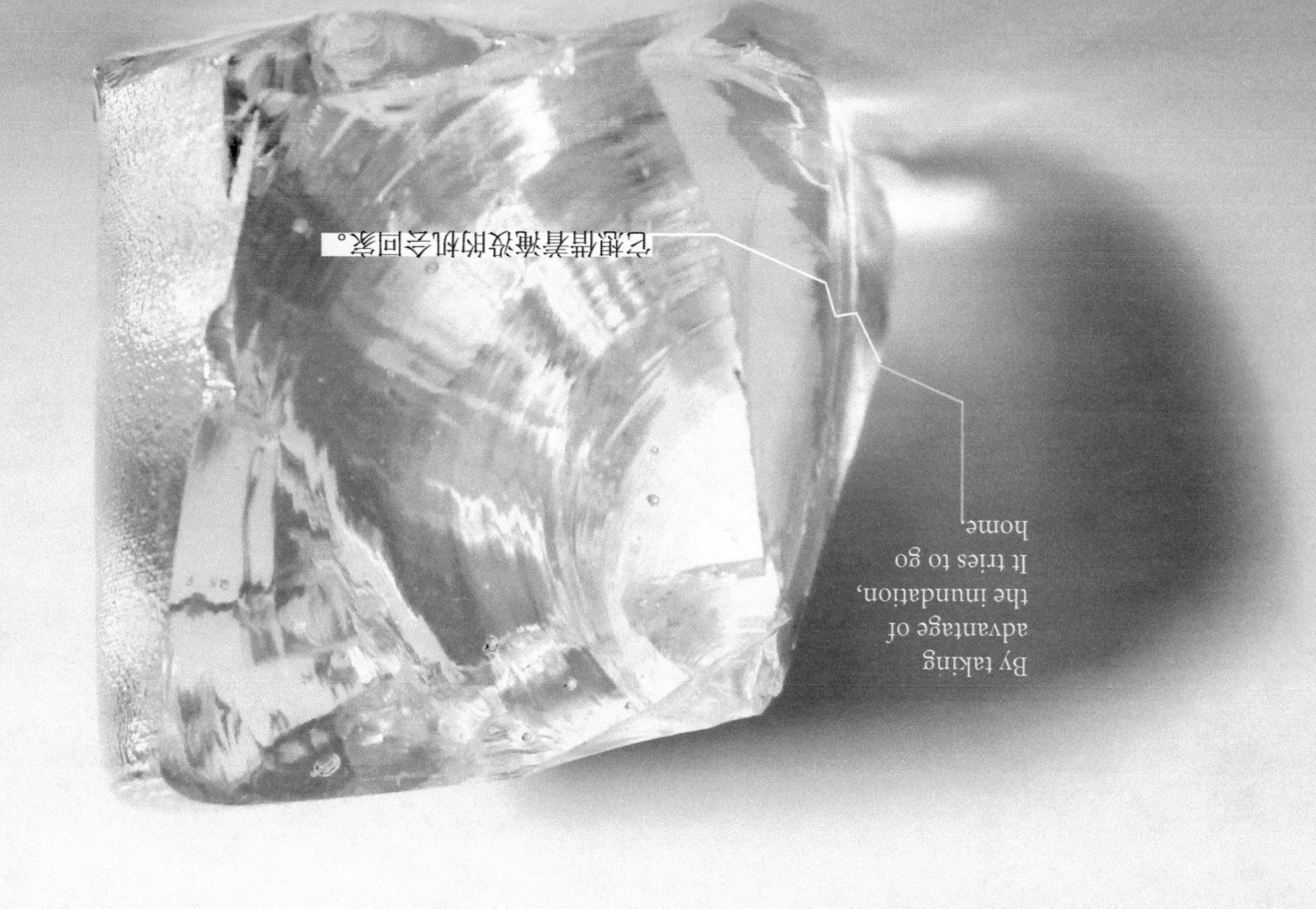

它趁洪水泛滥的时候会回家。

By taking
advantage of
the inundation,
It tries to go
home.

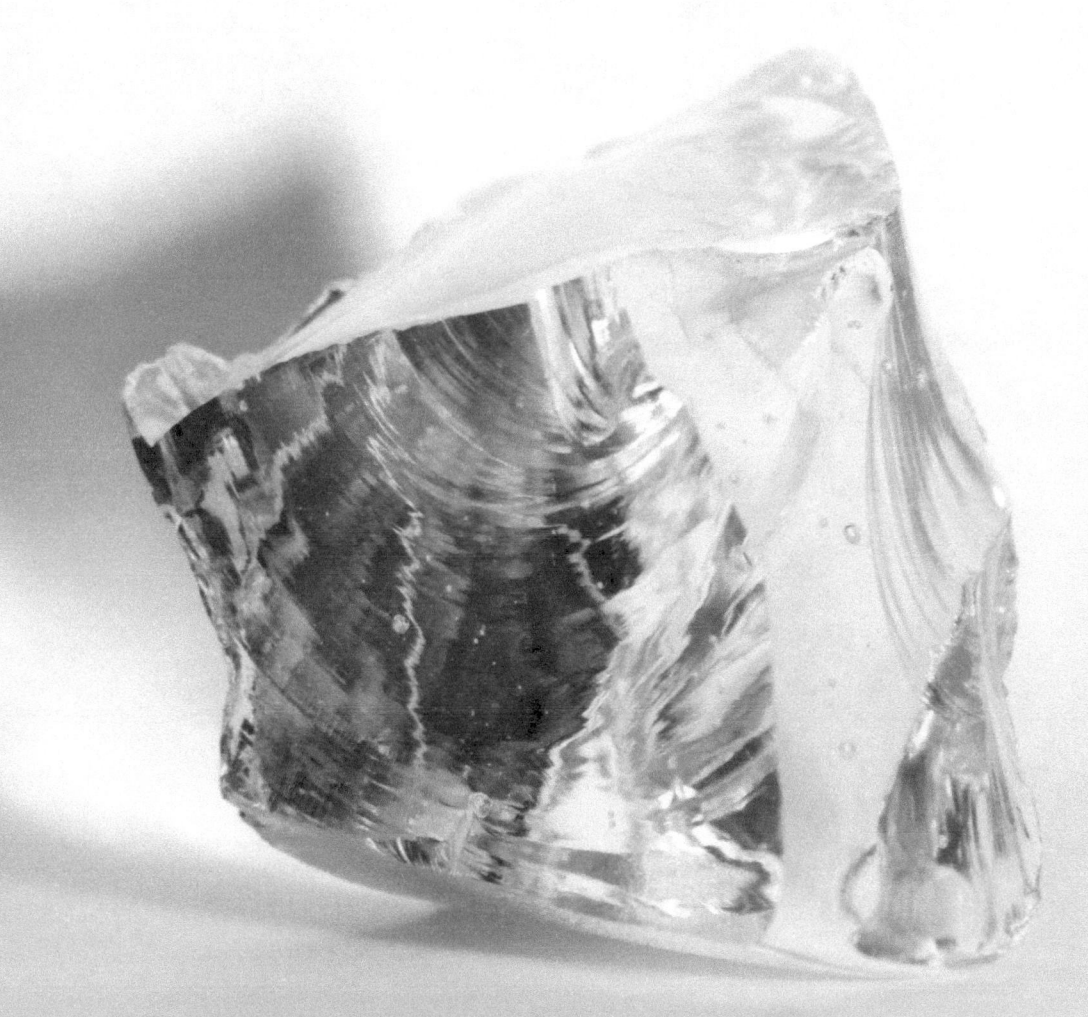

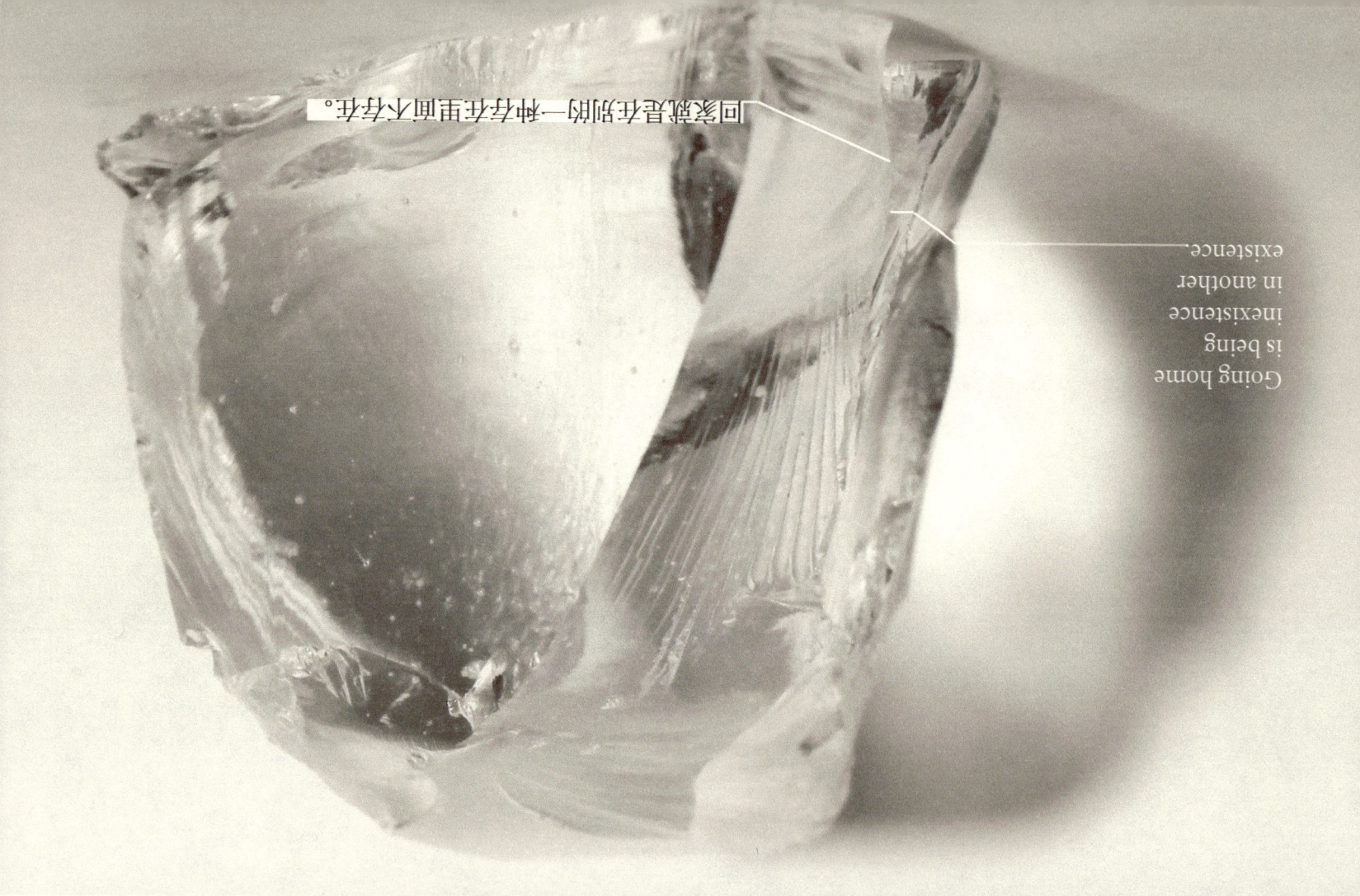

回家就是在别处——种存在里的不存在。

Going home is being inexistence in another existence.

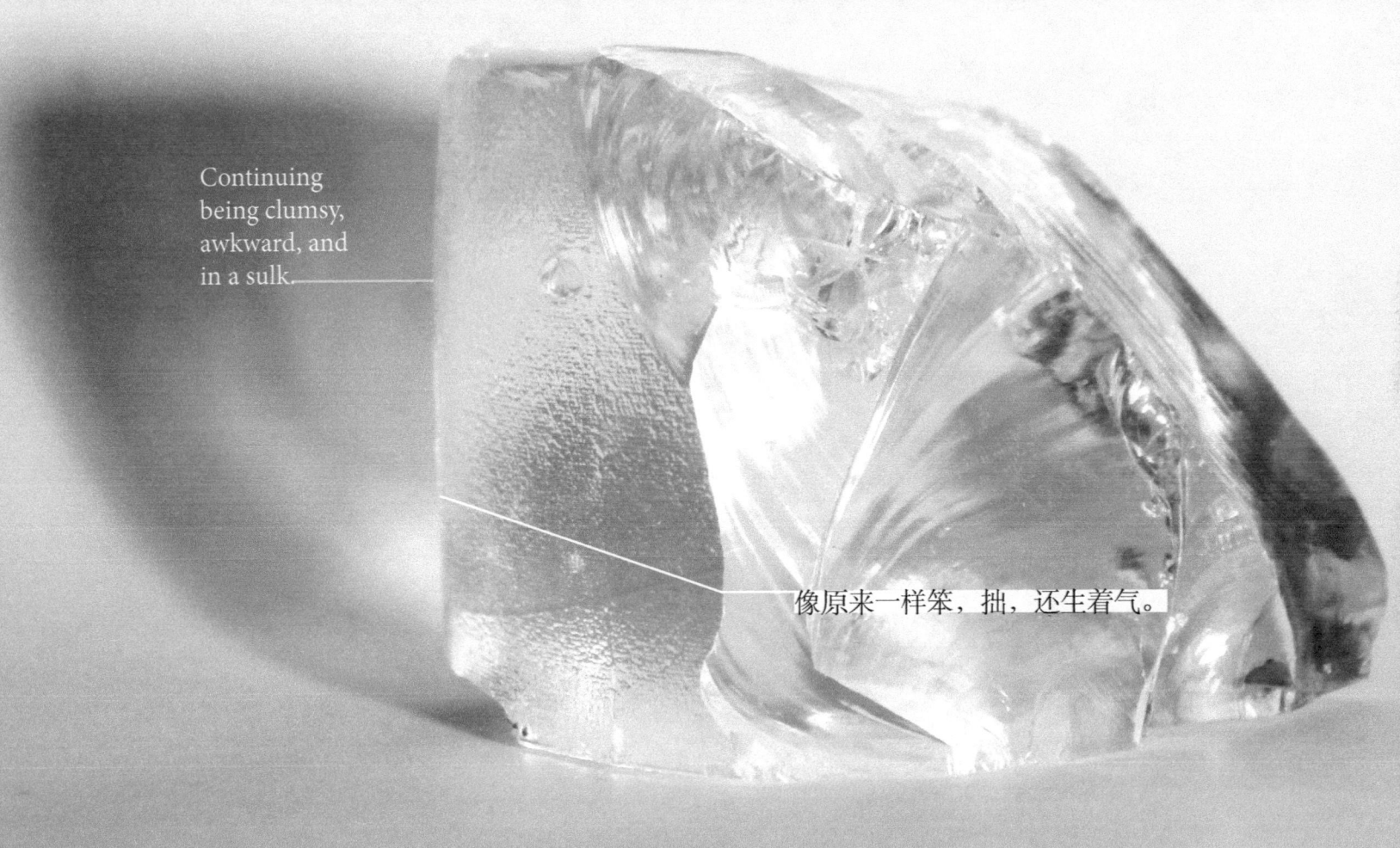

Continuing
being clumsy,
awkward, and
in a sulk.

像原来一样笨，拙，还生着气。

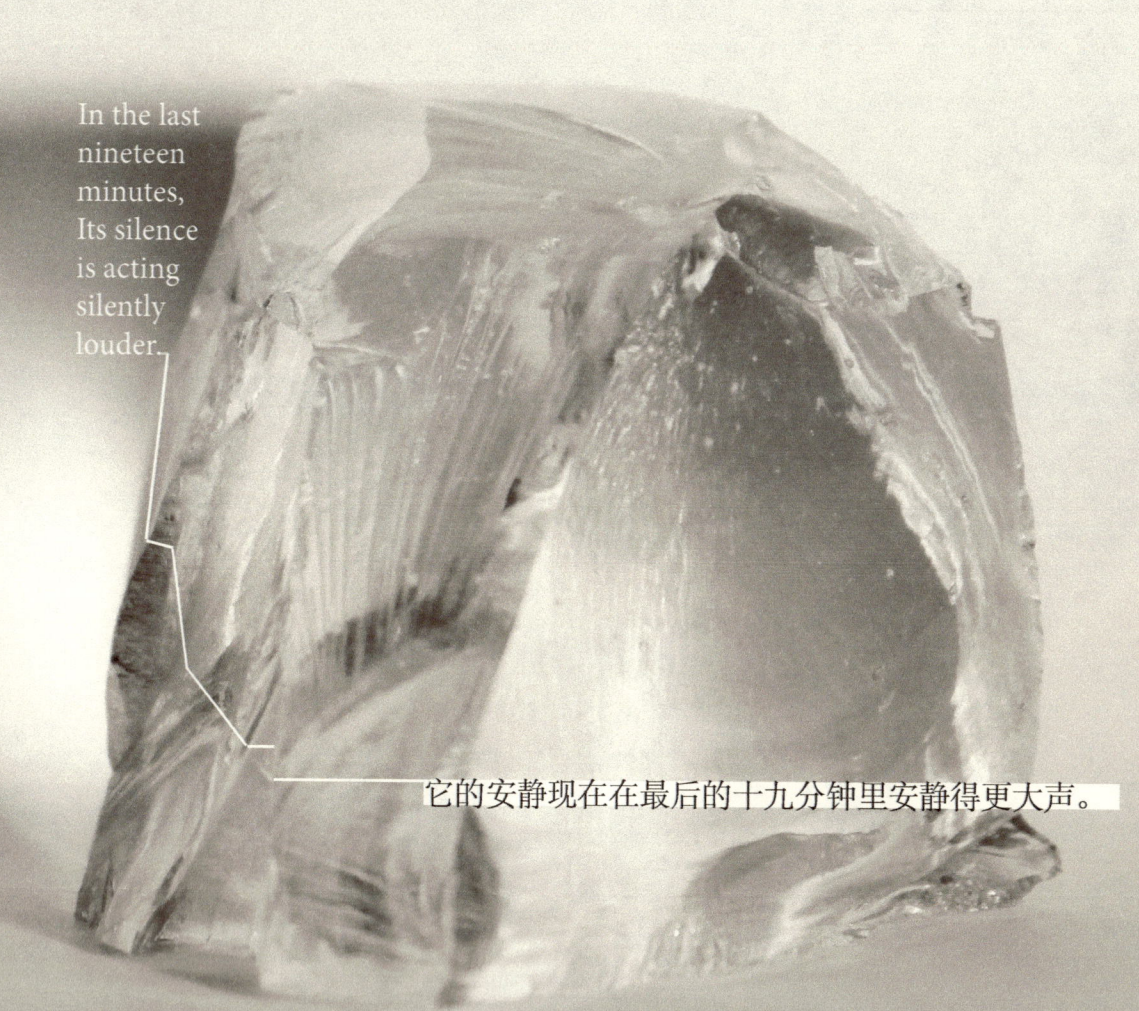

In the last
nineteen
minutes,
Its silence
is acting
silently
louder.

它的安静现在在最后的十九分钟里安静得更大声。

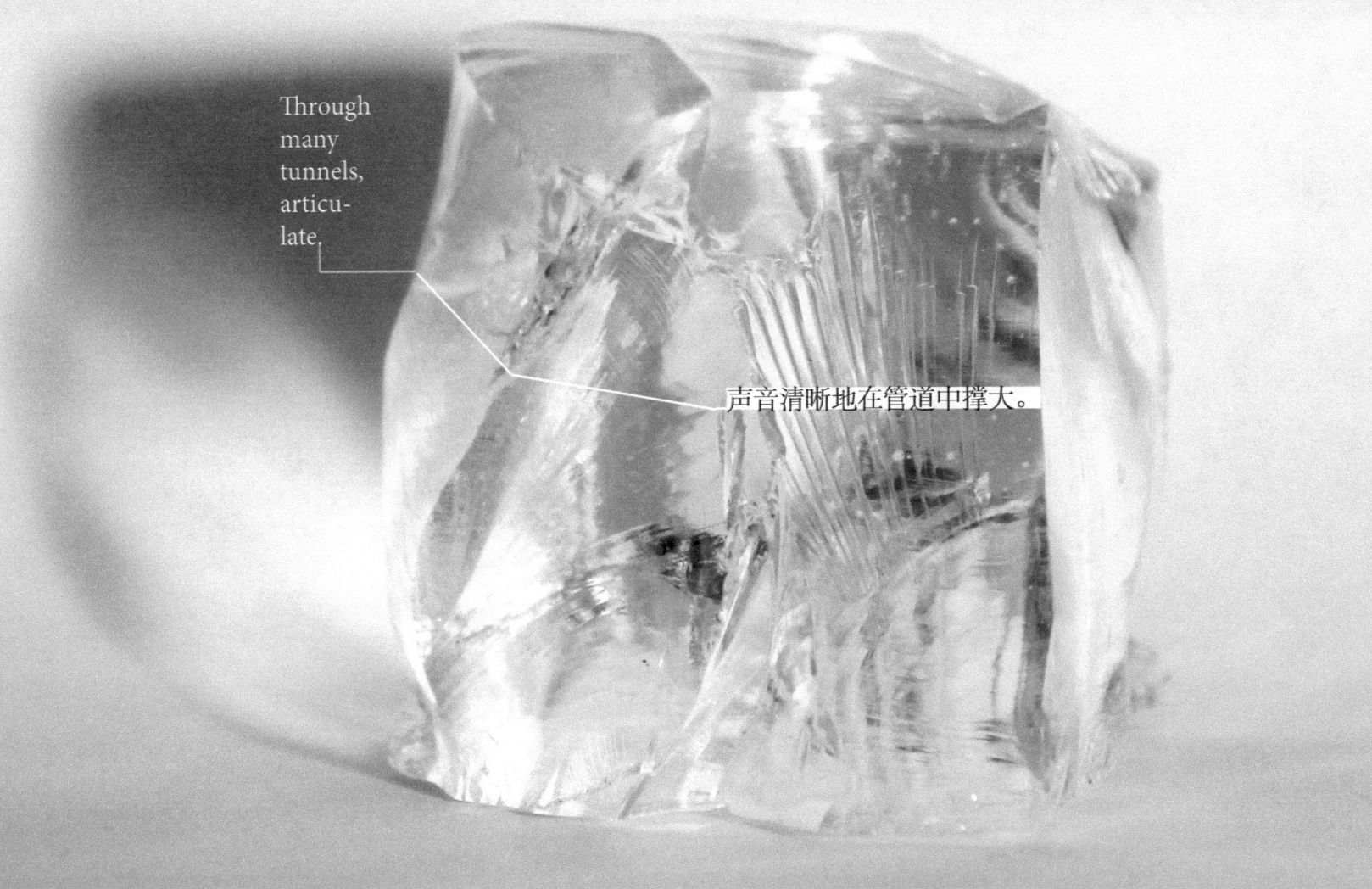

Through
many
tunnels,
articu-
late.

声音清晰地在管道中撑大。

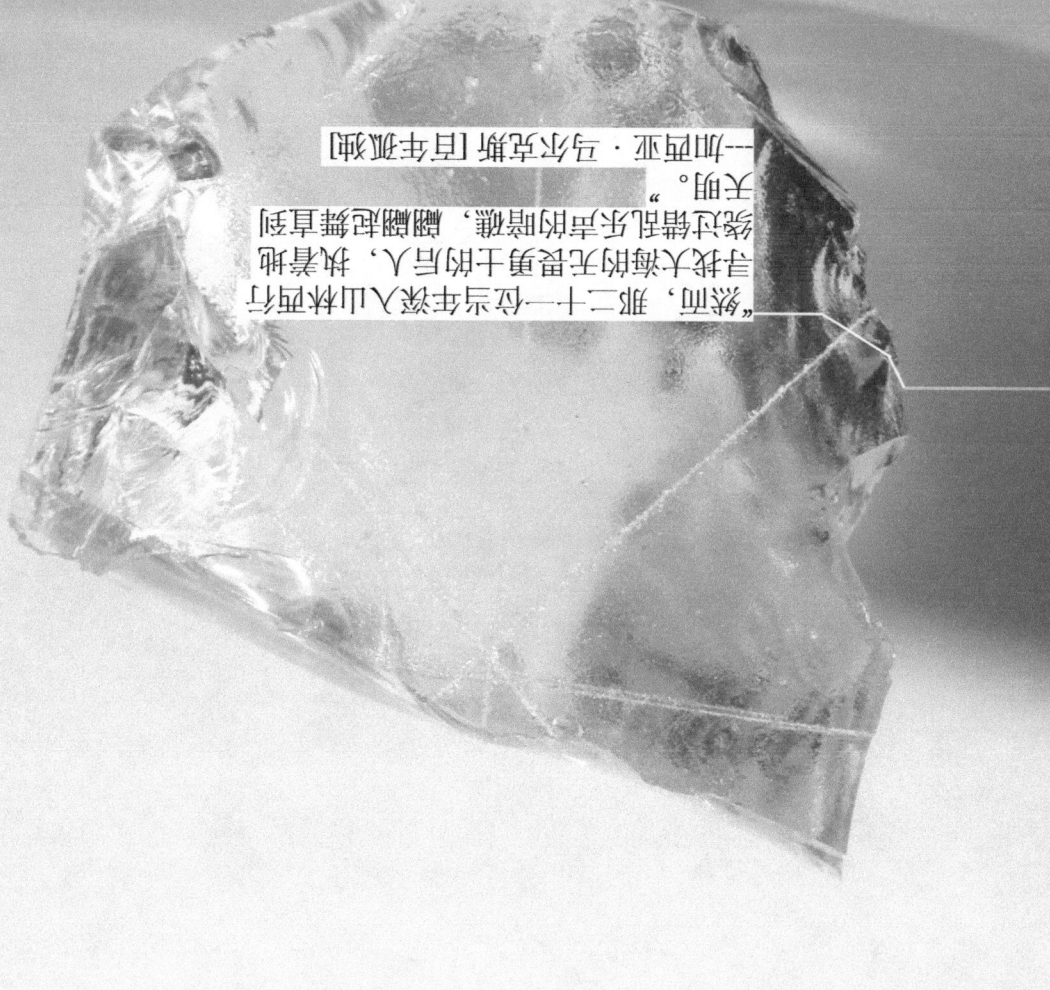

"But the stubborn descendants of the twenty-one intrepid people who plowed through the mountains in search of the sea to the west avoided the reefs of the melodic mixup and the dancing went on until dawn."
Gabriel Garcia Marquez, *One Hundred Years of Solitude*

"然而，那二十一位勇者后人又坚持行穿越大海的无尽黄土的后人，执着地躲过错乱无序的暗礁，翩翩起舞直到天明。"
——加西亚·马尔克斯［百年孤独］

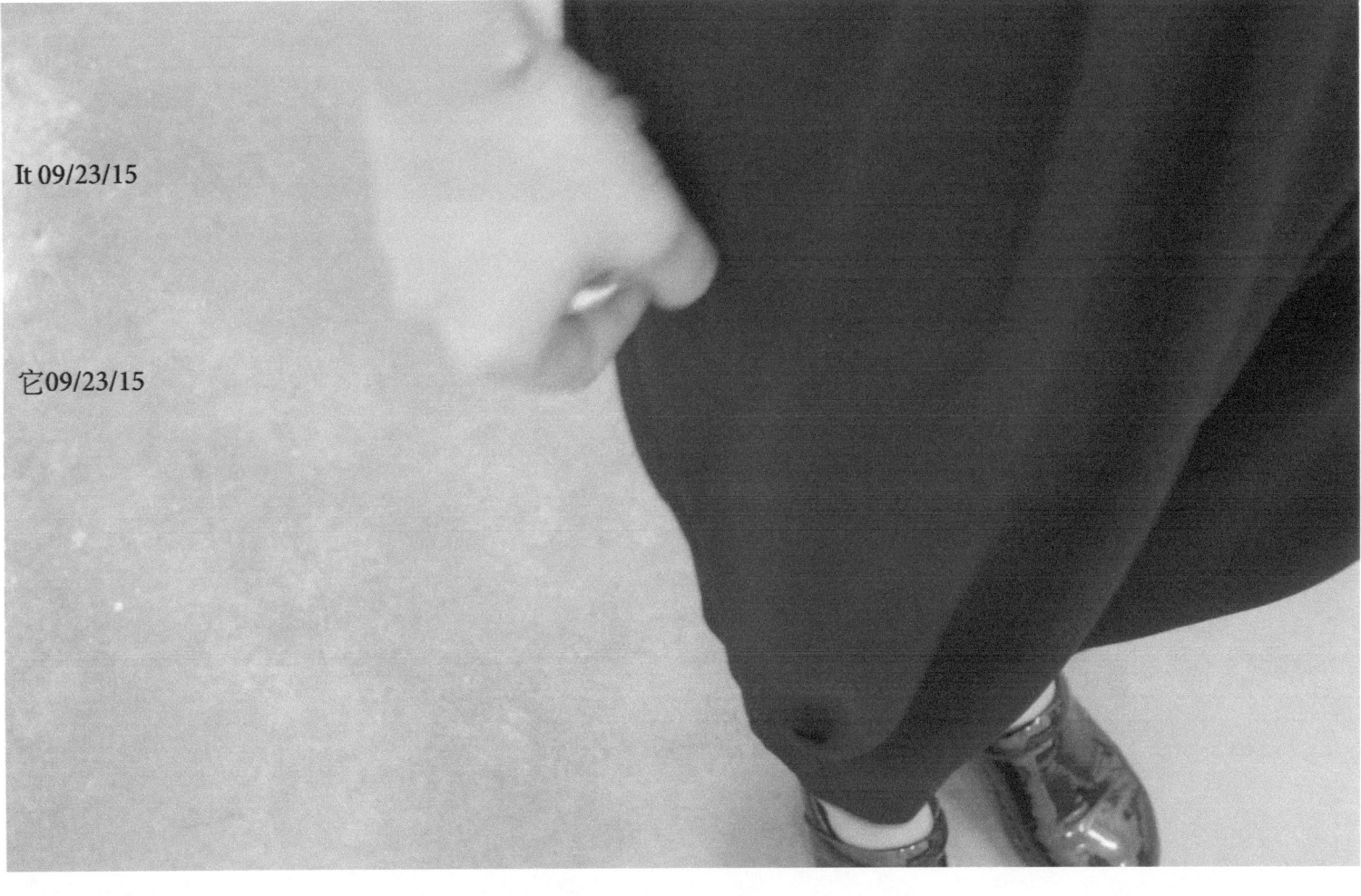

It 09/23/15

它09/23/15

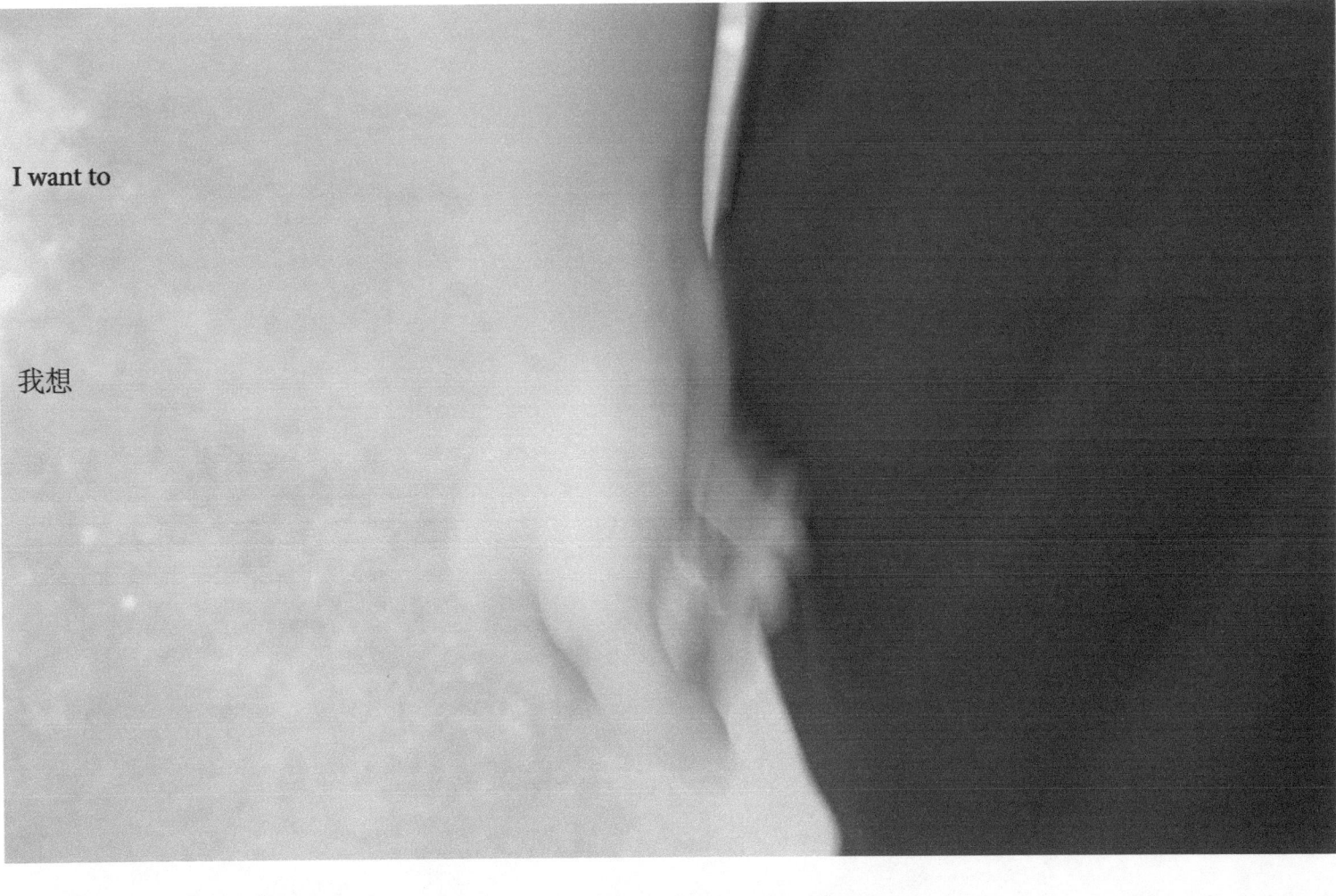

I want to

我想

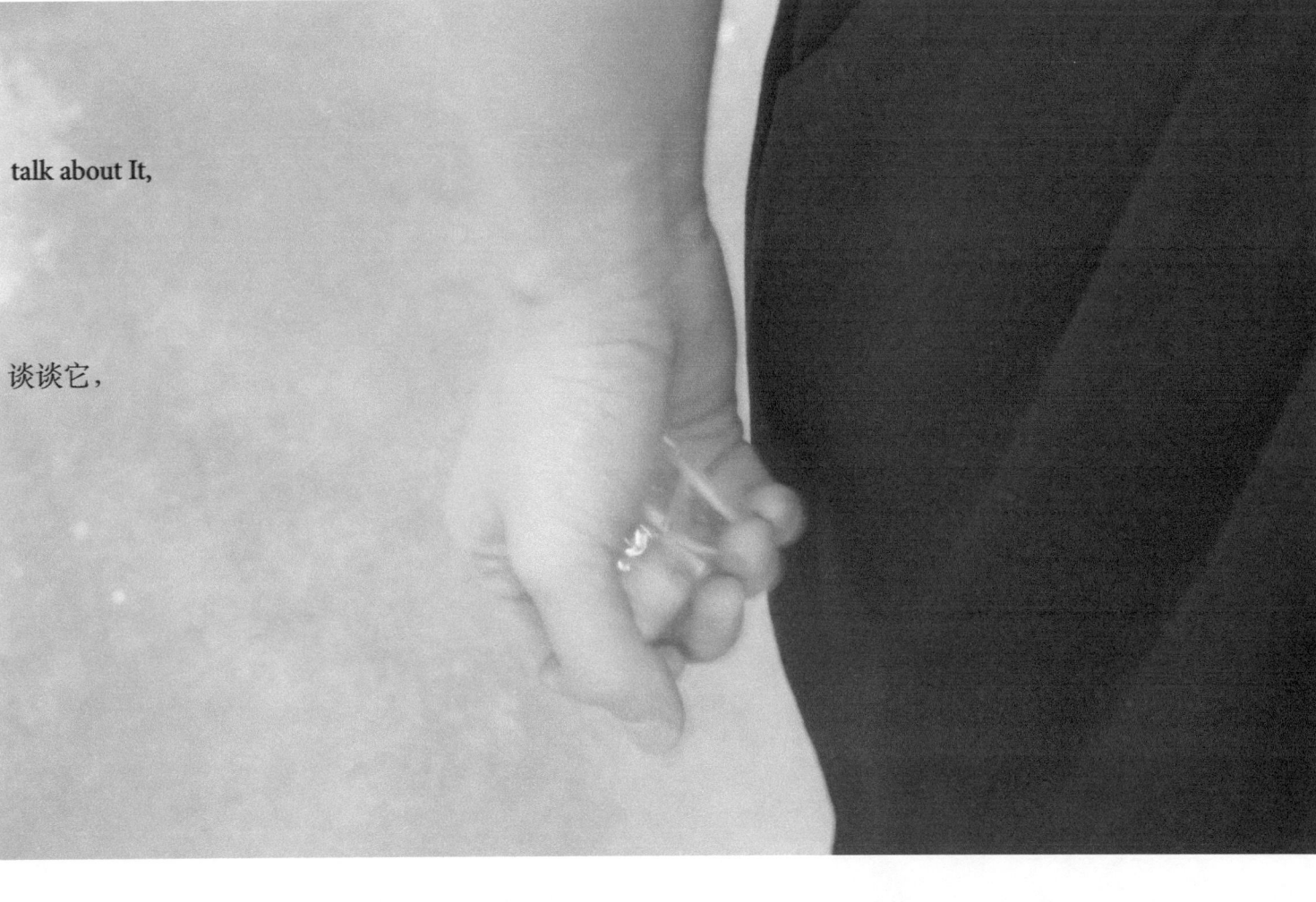

talk about It,

谈谈它，

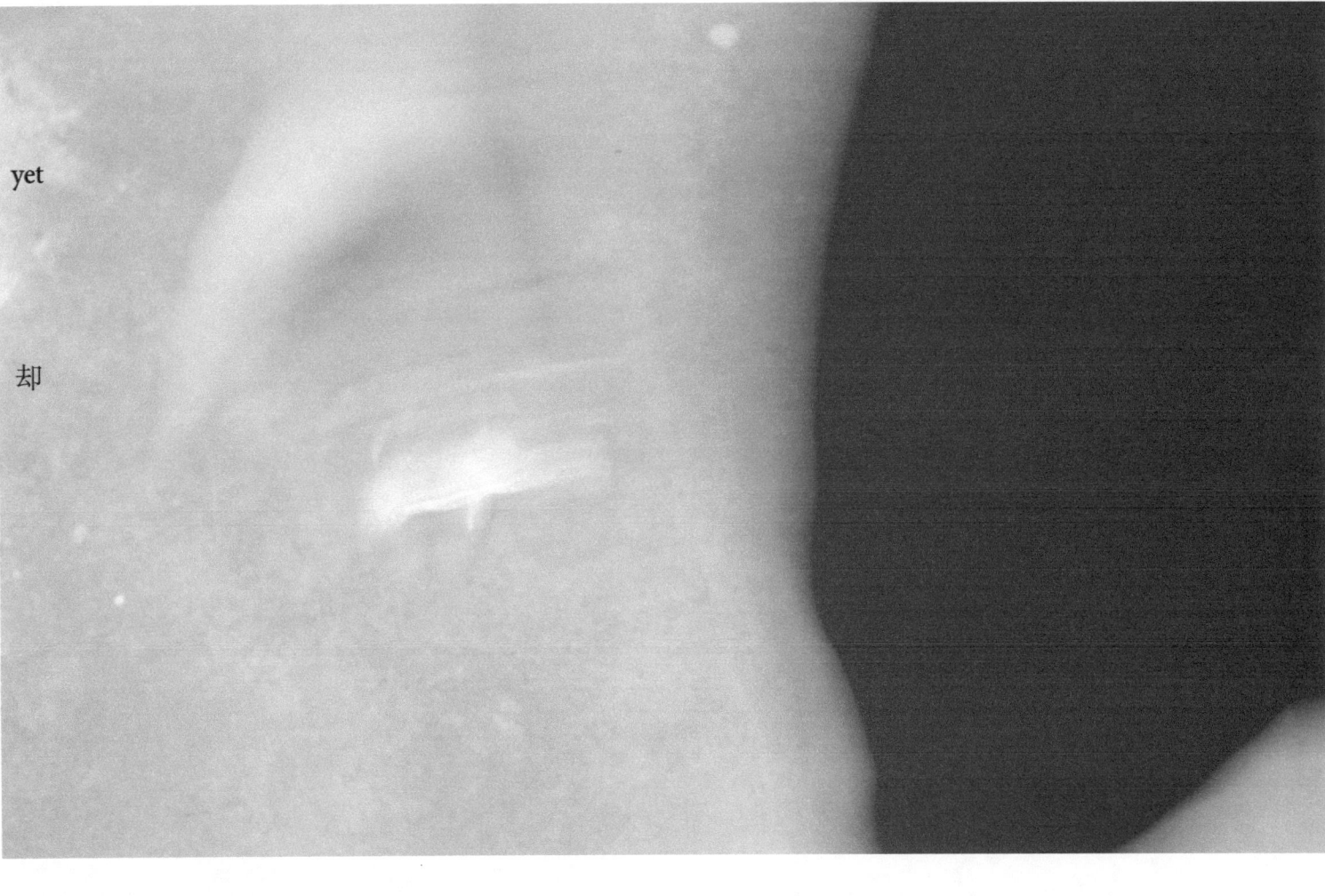

yet

却

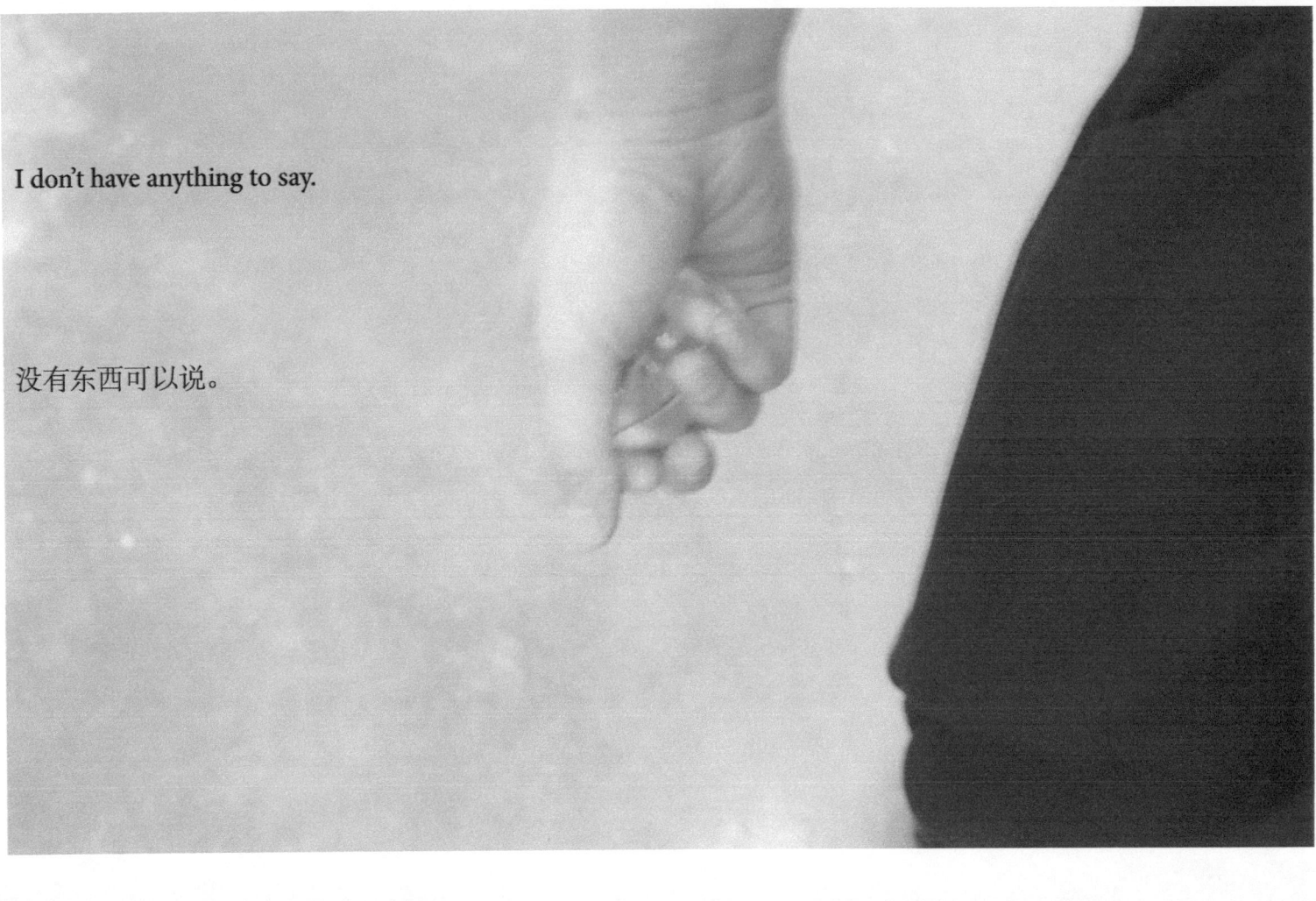

I don't have anything to say.

没有东西可以说。

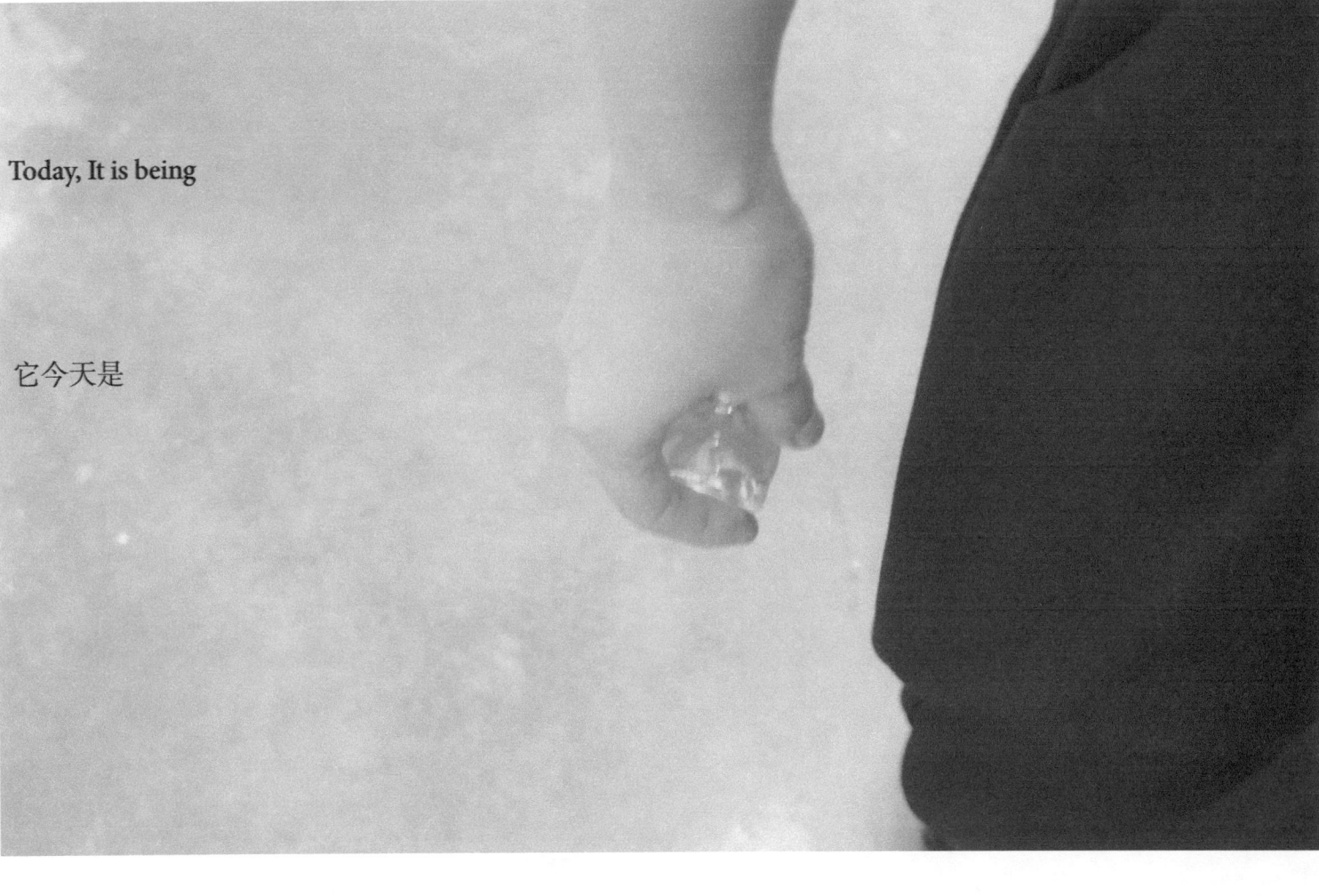

Today, It is being

它今天是

a small animal dwells in my right hand.

寄居在我右手的一只小动物。

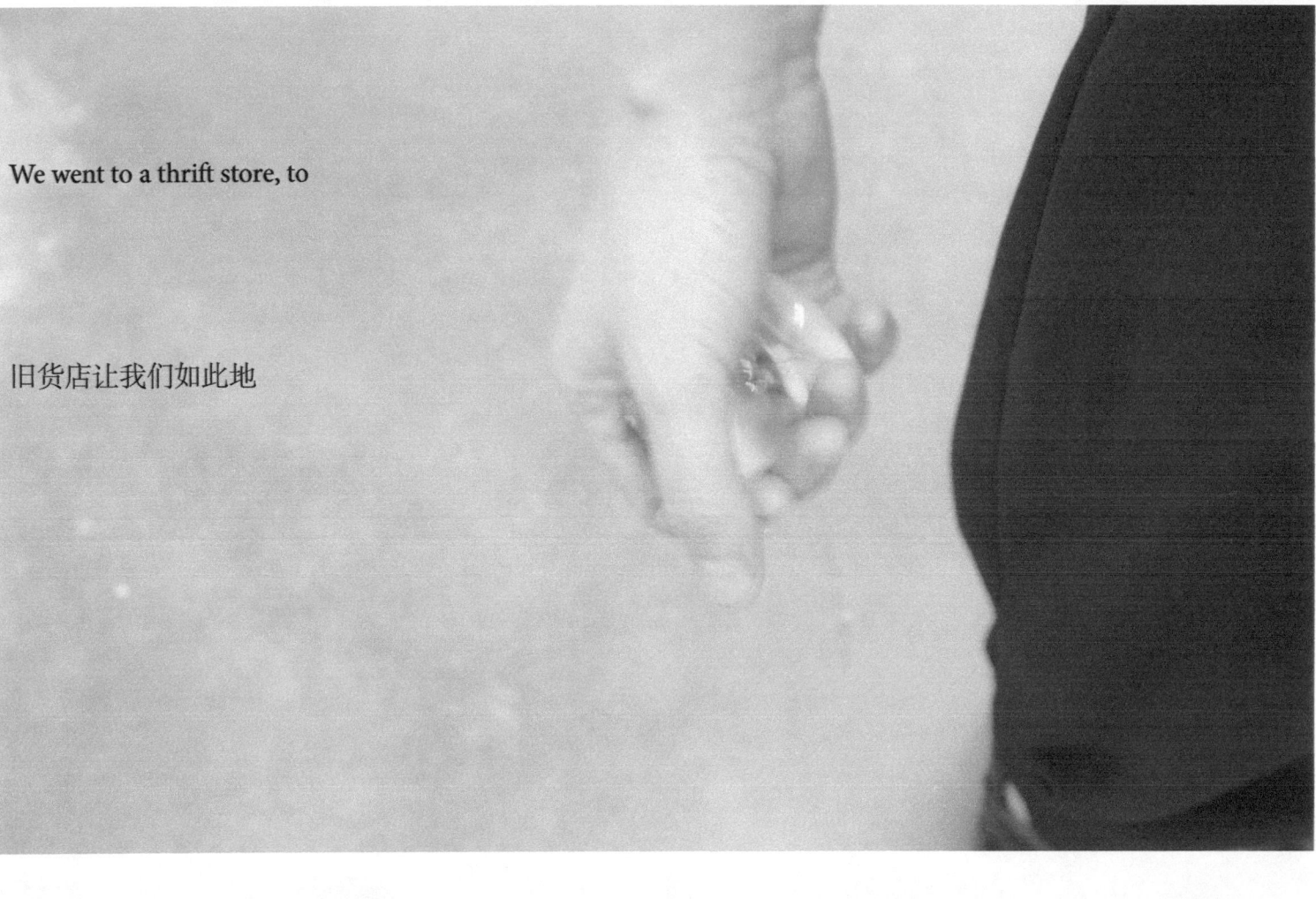

We went to a thrift store, to

旧货店让我们如此地

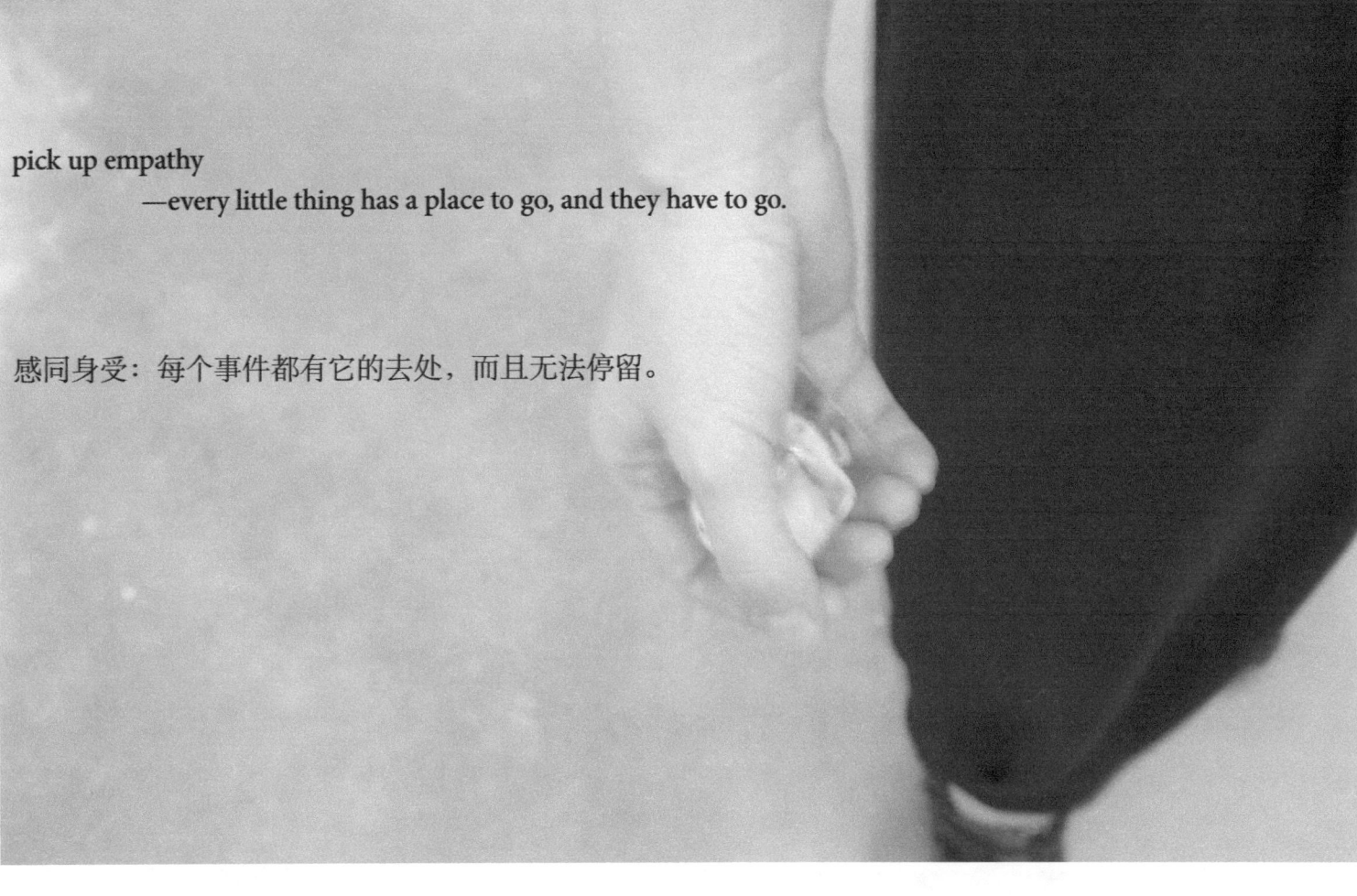

pick up empathy
     —every little thing has a place to go, and they have to go.

感同身受：每个事件都有它的去处，而且无法停留。

Go, go, go.

步履不停。

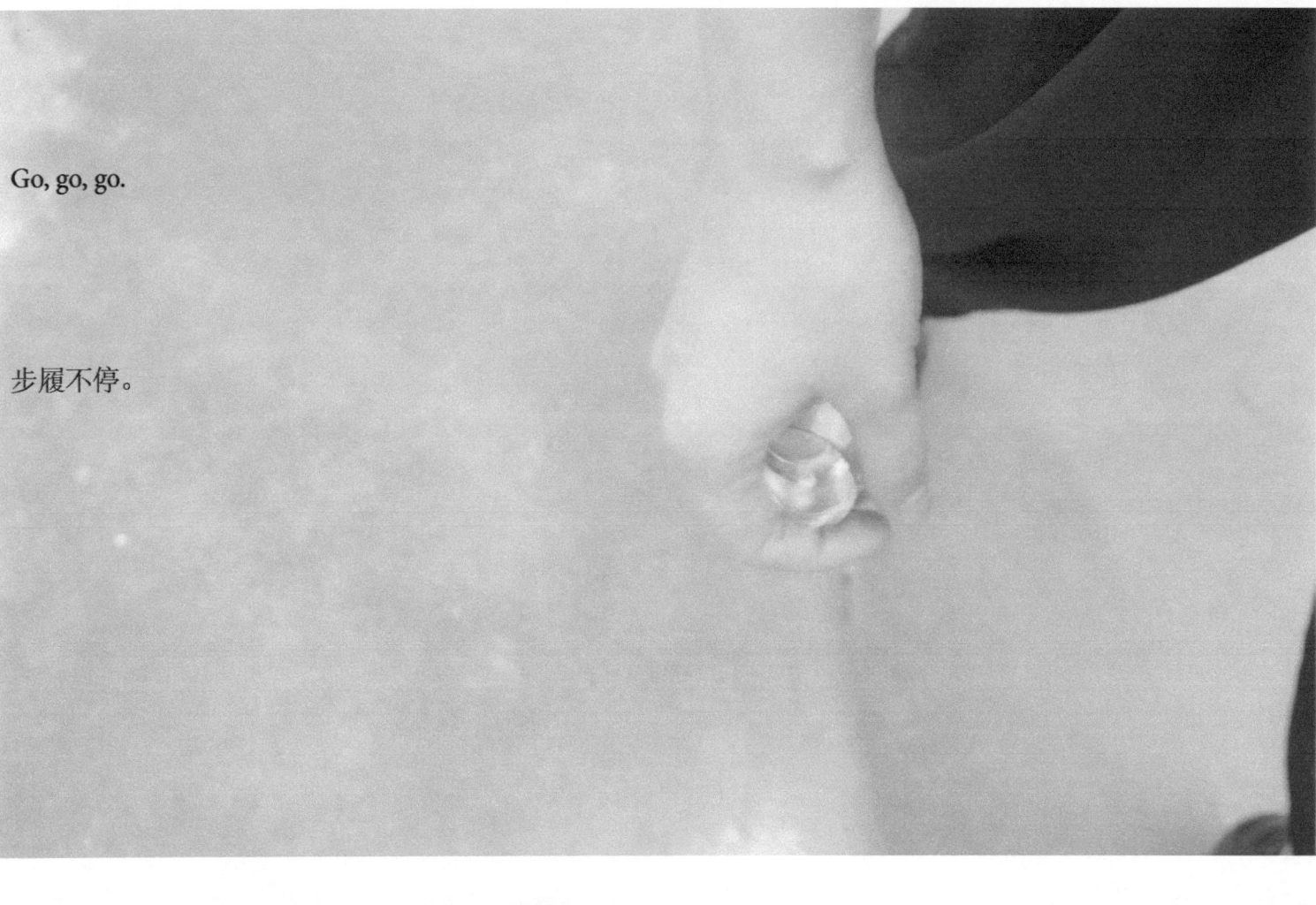

People go to encounter,

人和人相遇，

faces go to melt,

脸与脸重叠,

and the present is made.

就成就了现在。

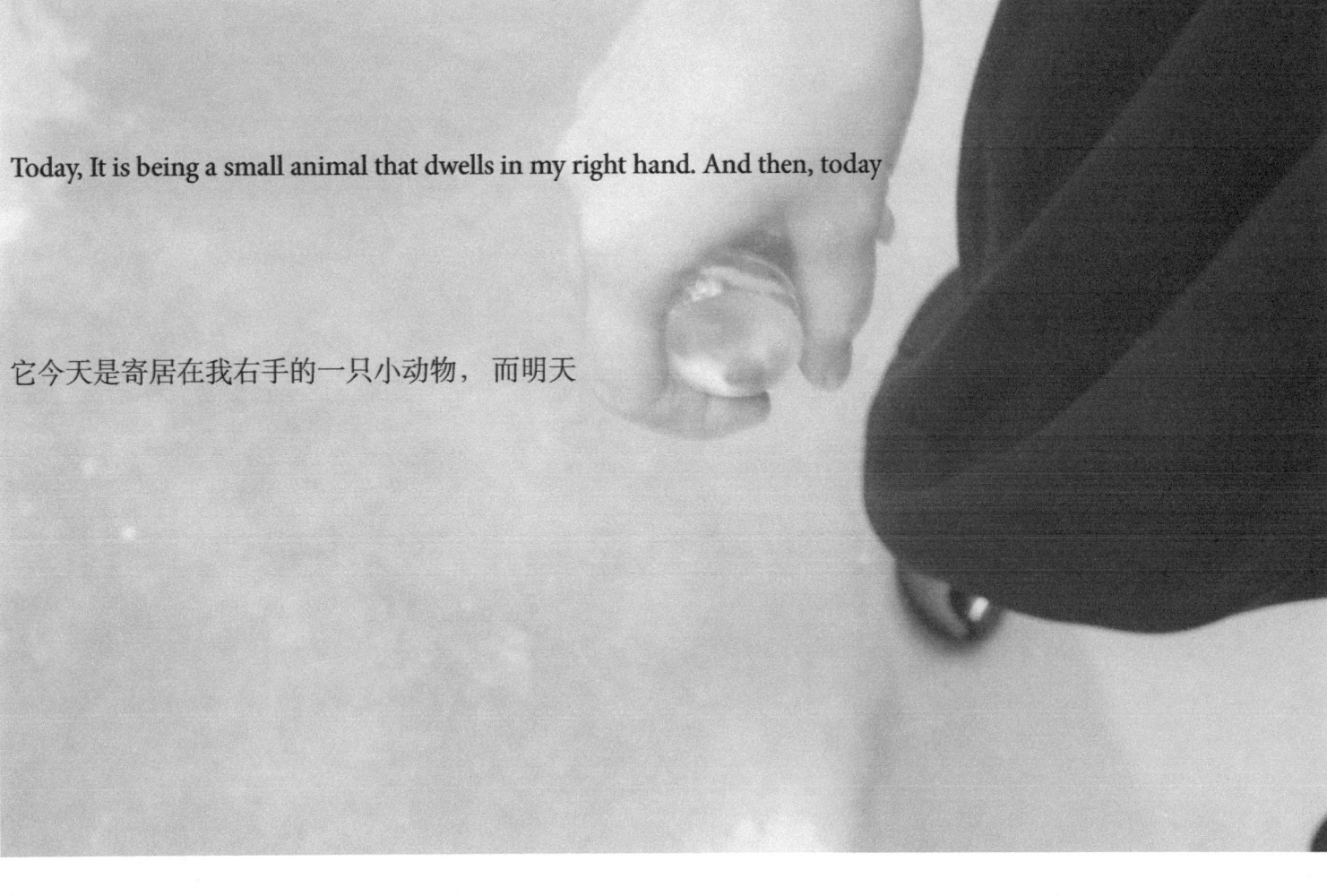

Today, It is being a small animal that dwells in my right hand. And then, today

它今天是寄居在我右手的一只小动物，而明天

has to go.

呢?

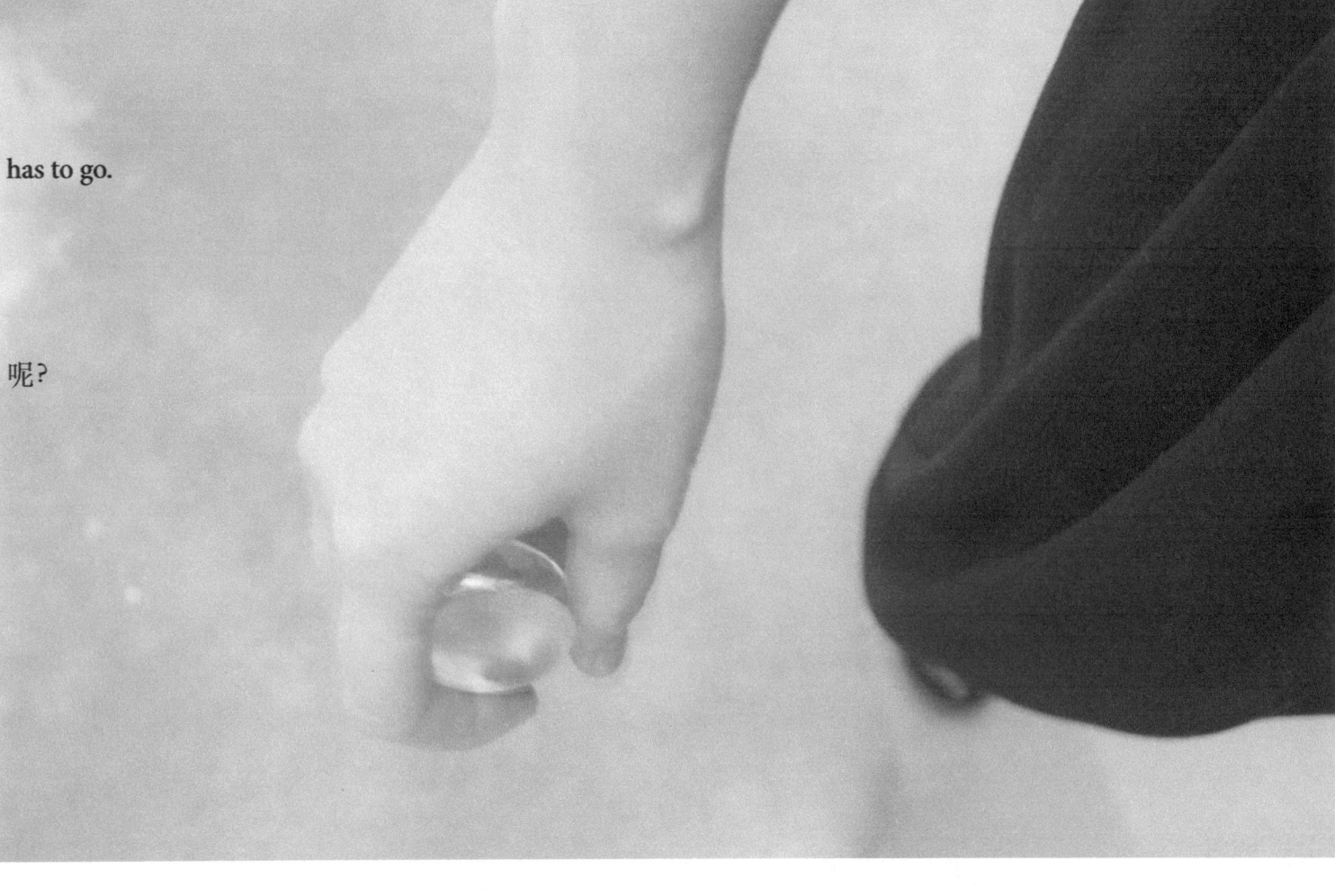

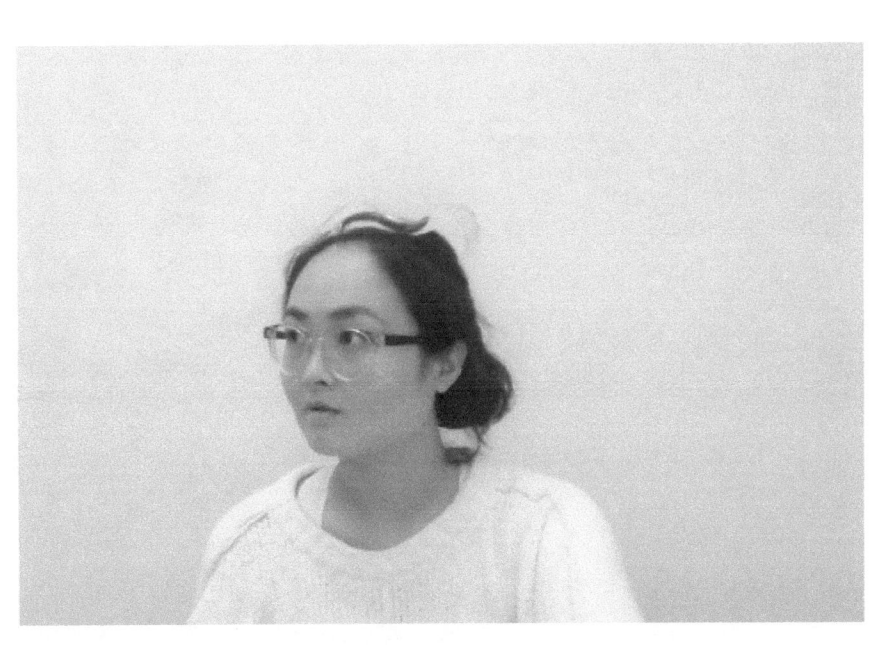

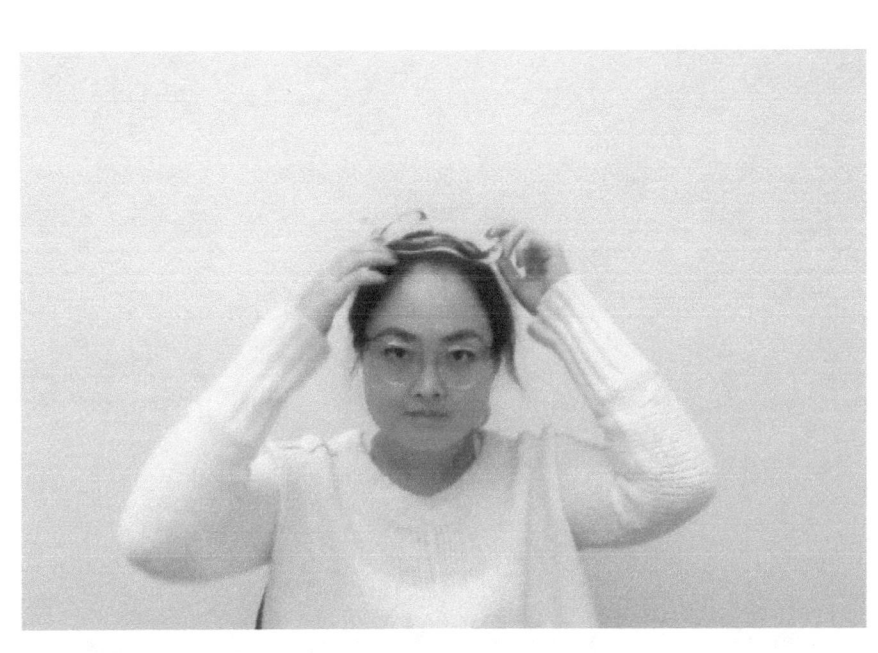

今天， Today,

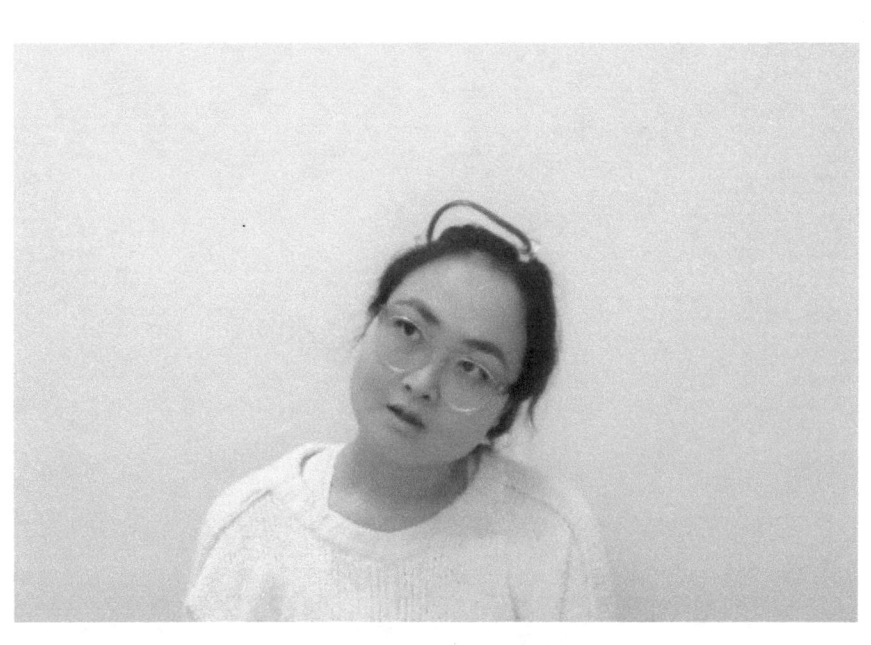

在 this

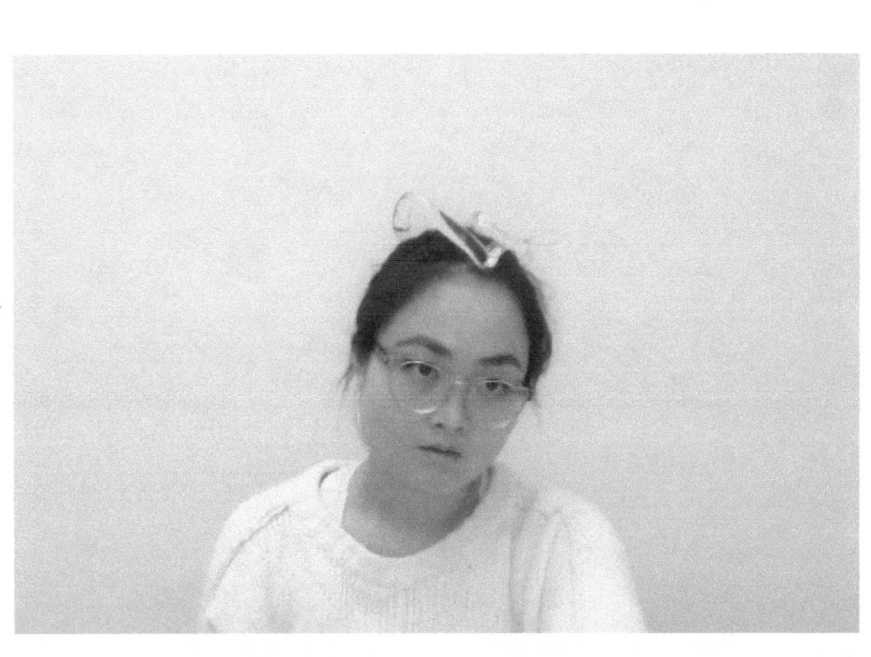

Thursday.

亥子不剃头。

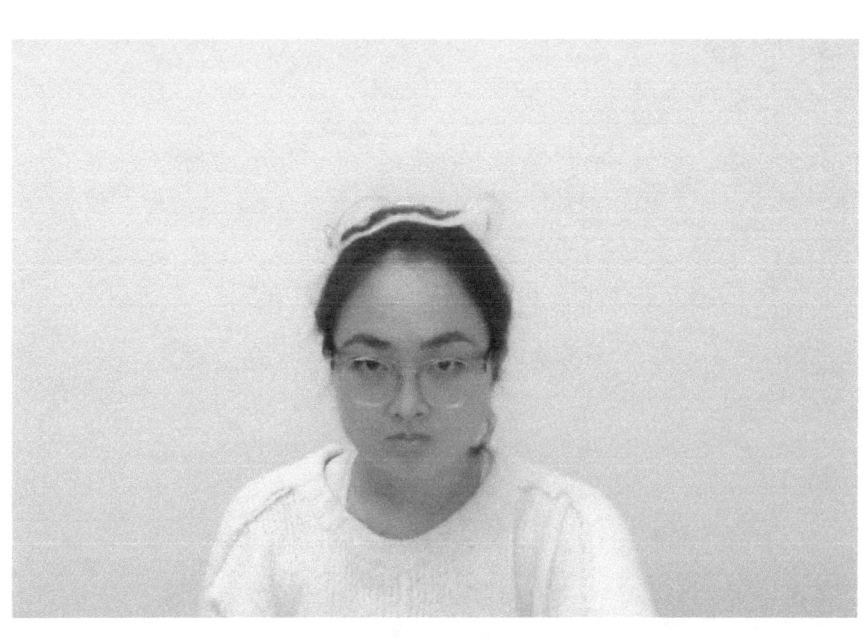

鳌輯

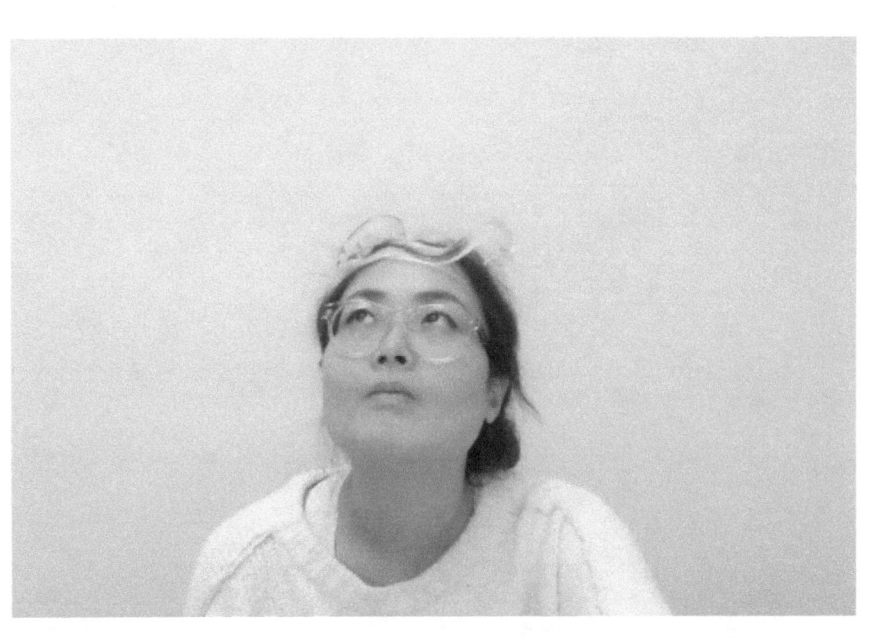

触摸，   Through

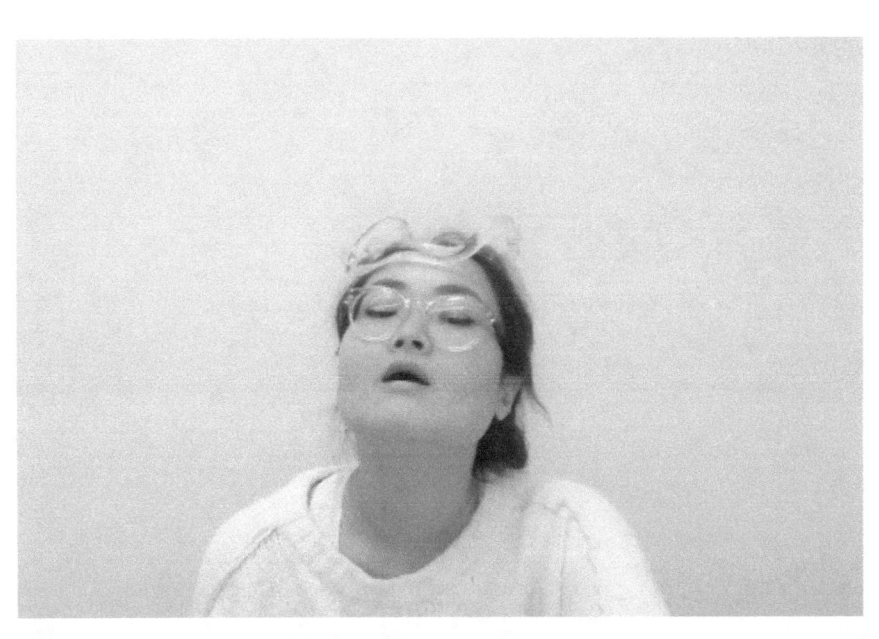

它来周游。   **touching,**

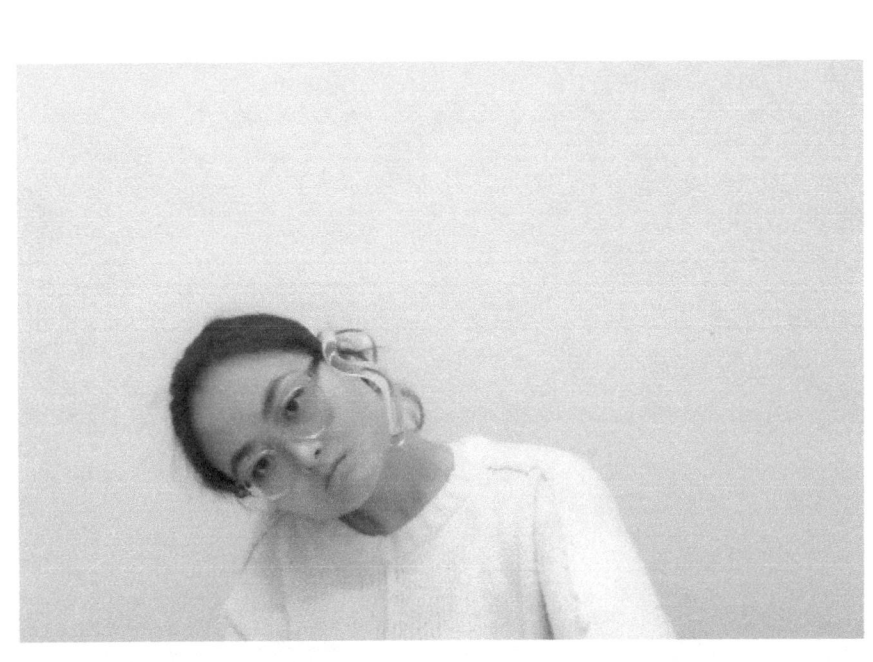

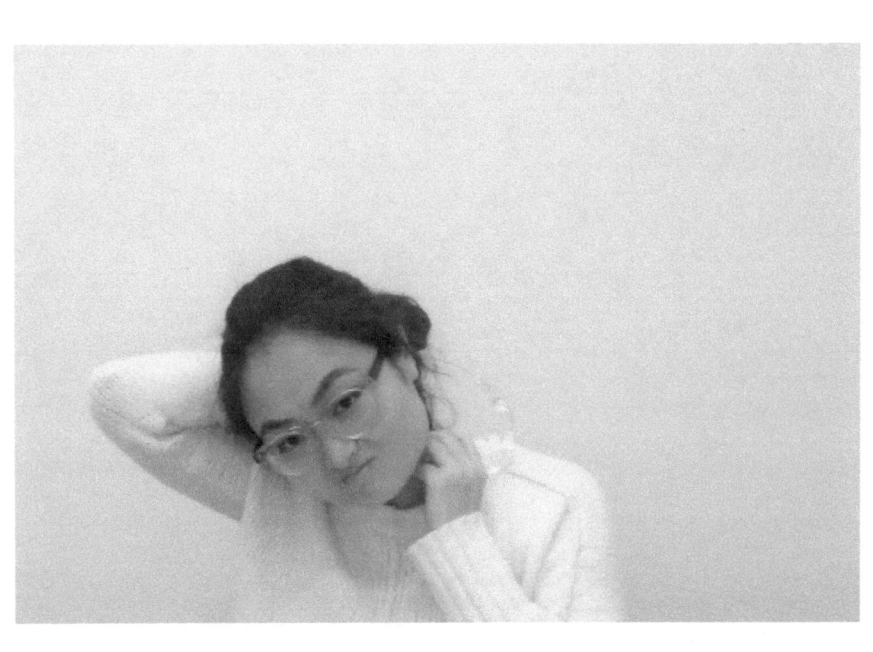

游丝，

travels.

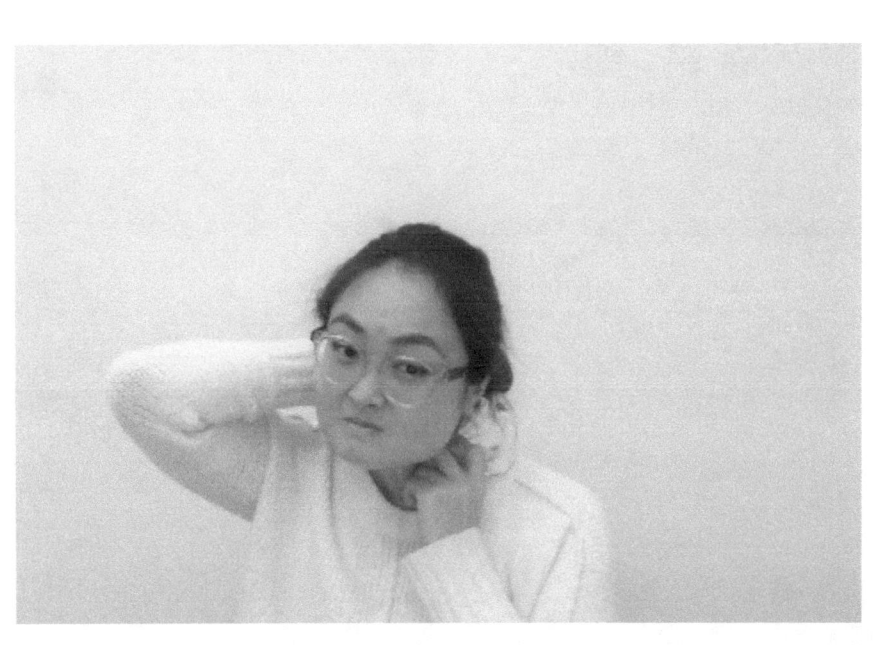

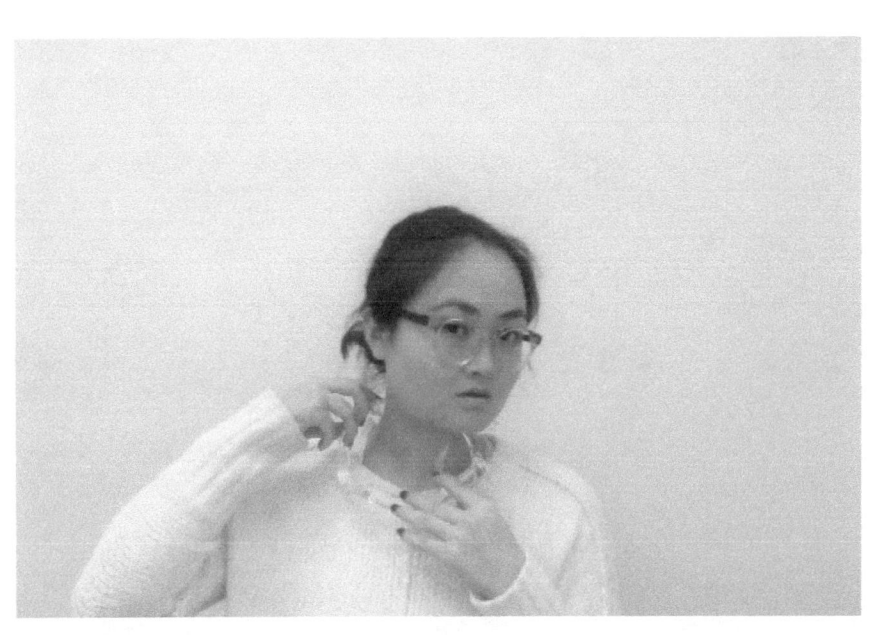

麻烦   To

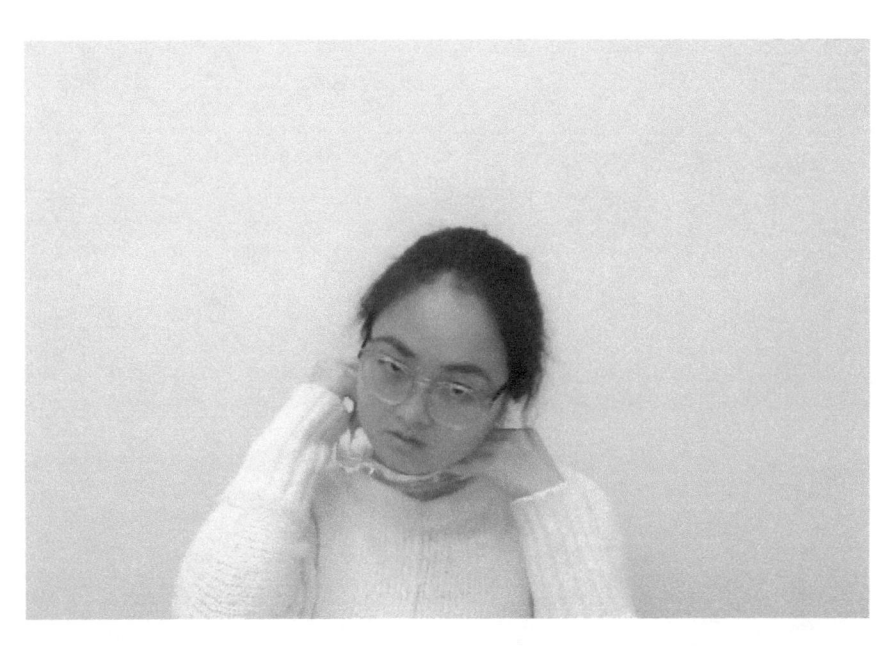

test,

[1]

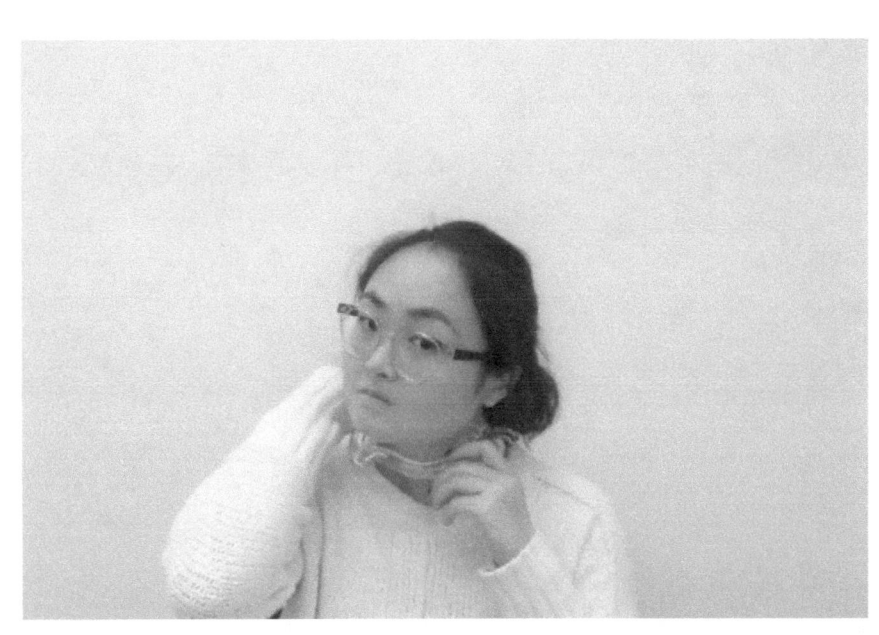

收事記,

ii

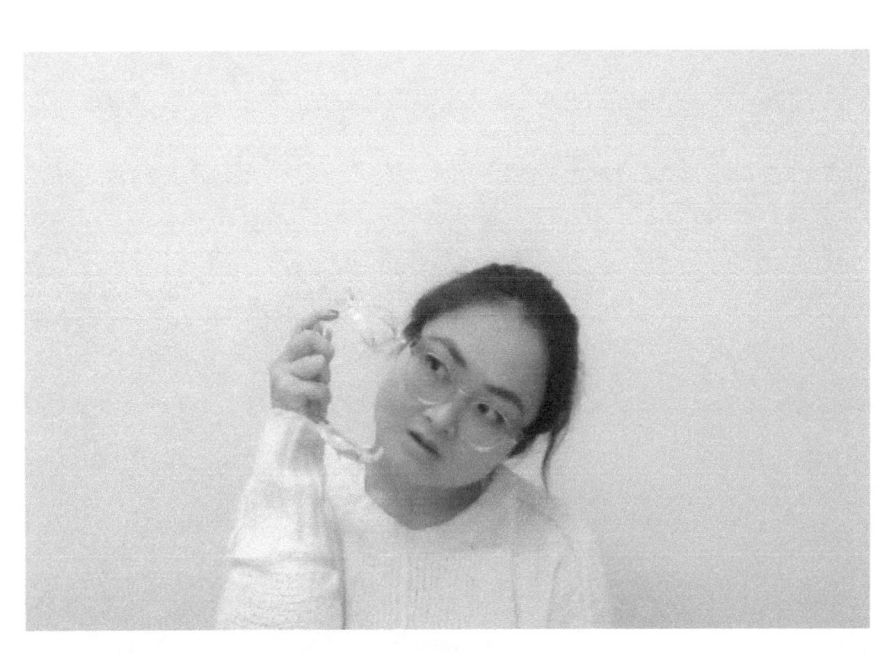

本末

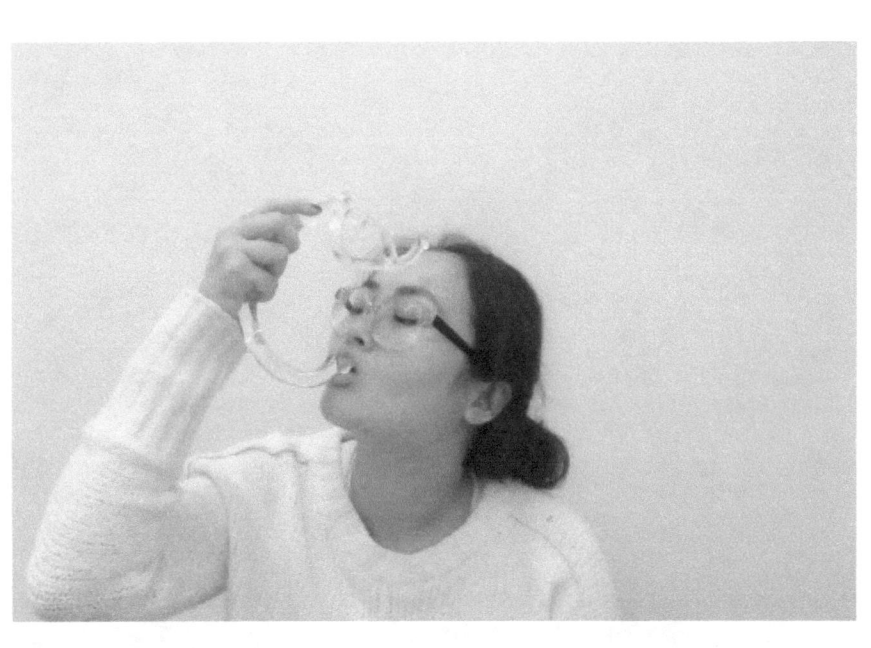

淡畦，

those

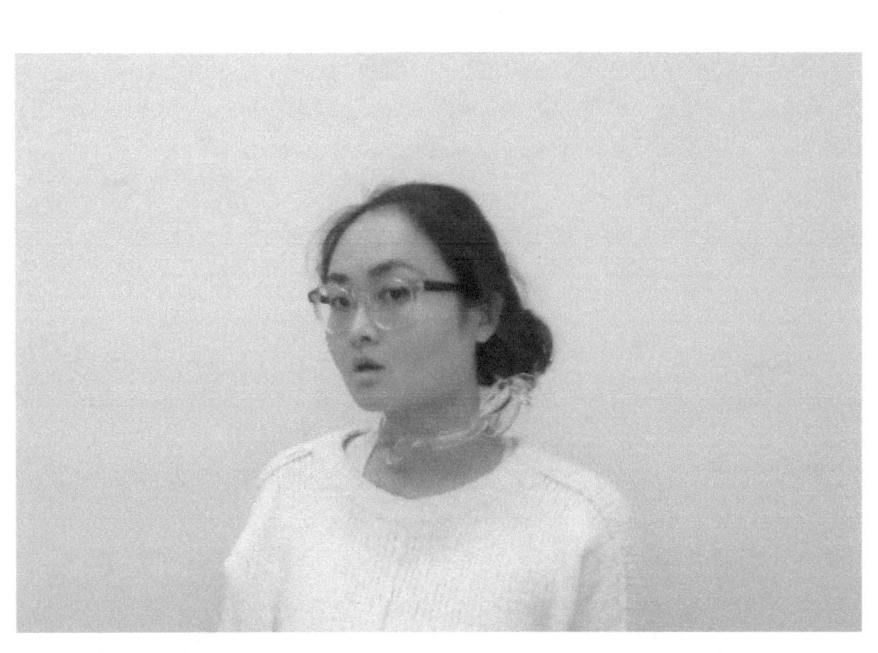

troubles

杜甫。

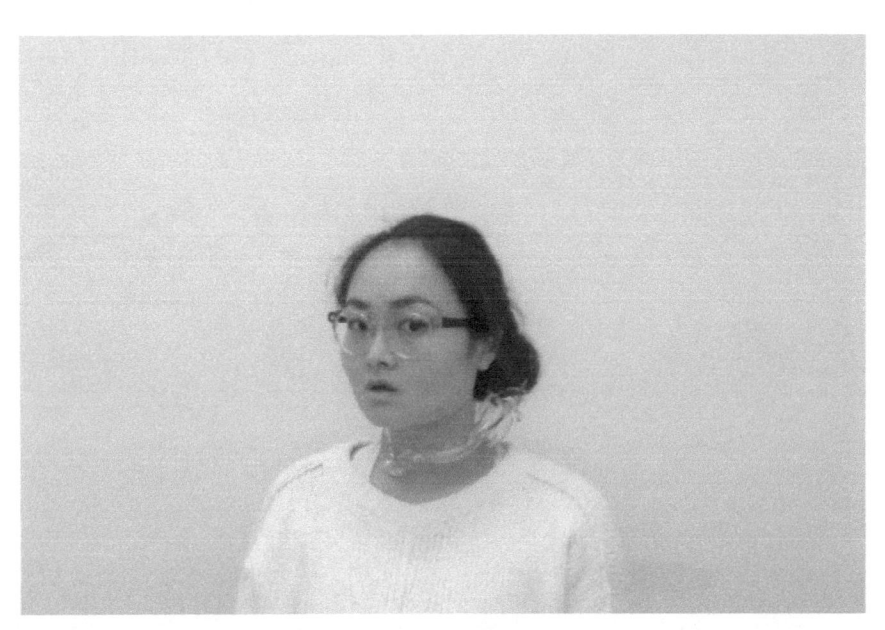

查查梦梦，

together.

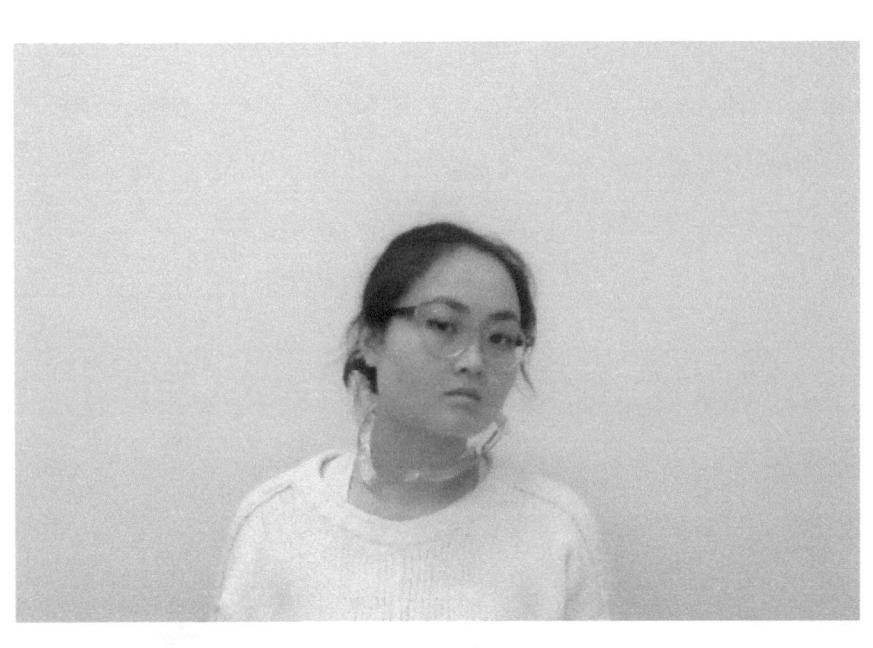

'Ɨ̵Ɨ̵₦₦

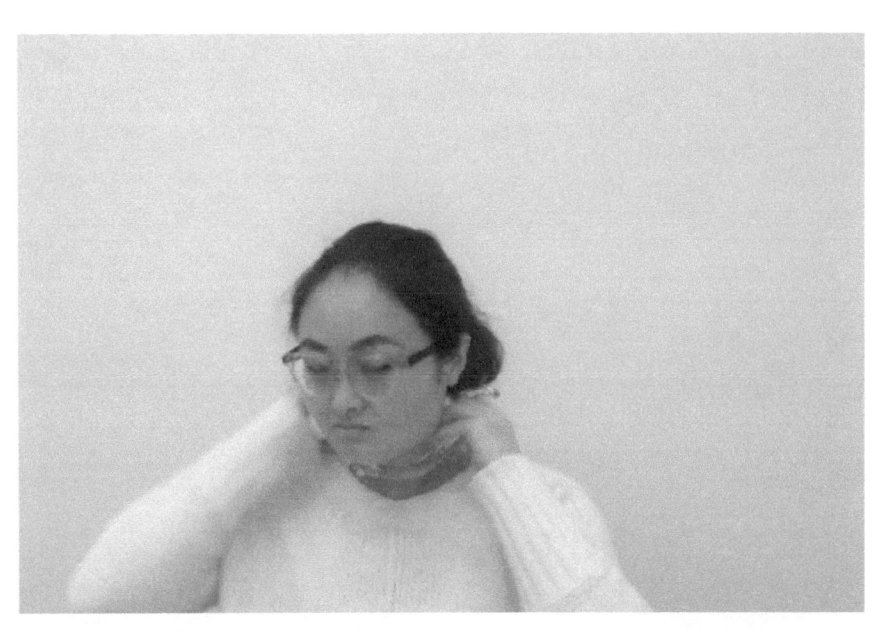

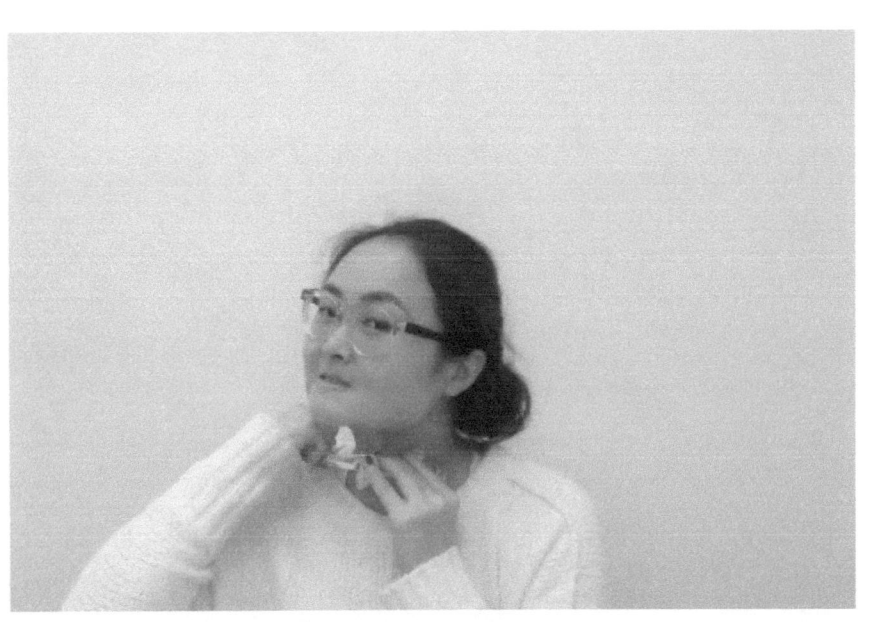

不到

tedious,

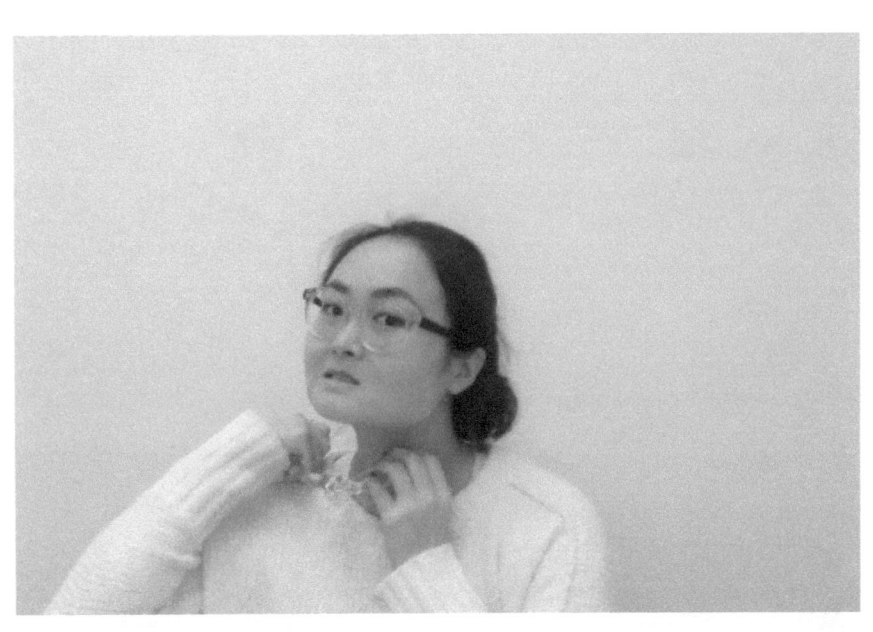

世紀。

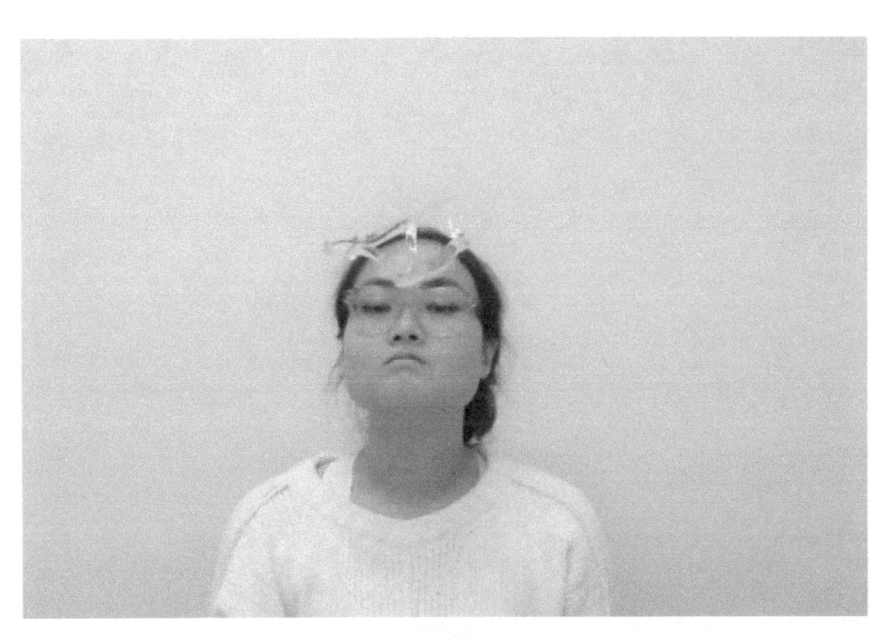

次日，   tidy,

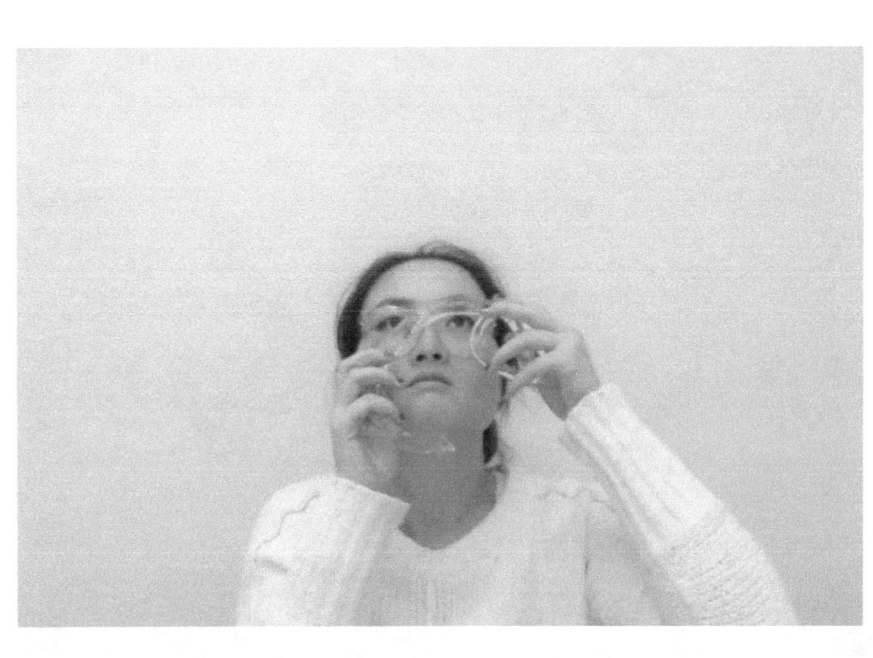

totally.

꿈

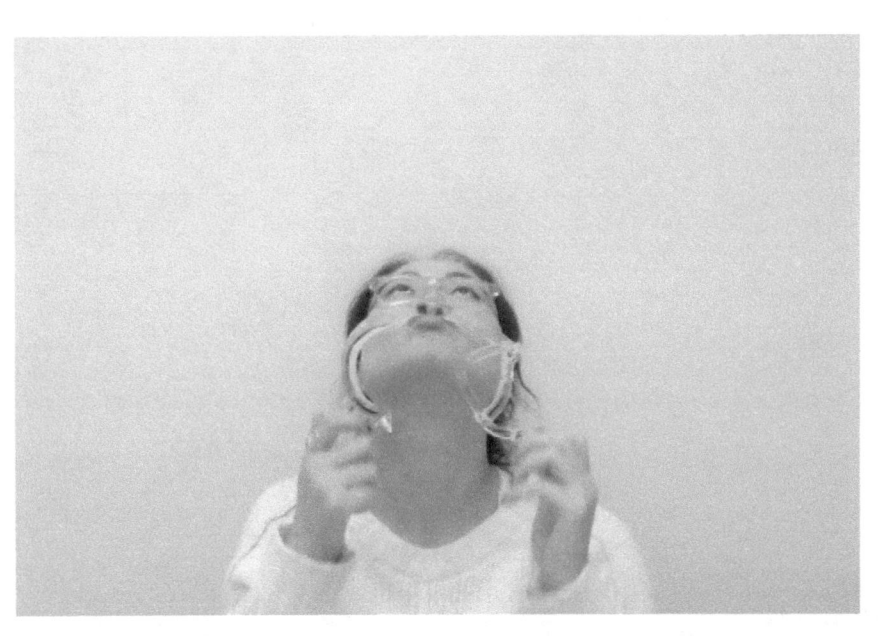

第一章書牌。

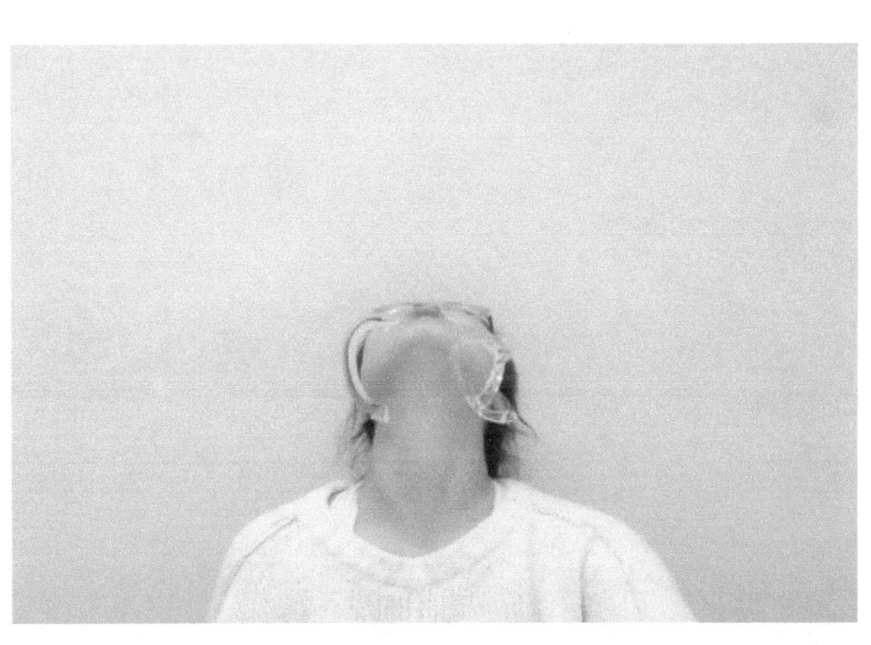

嘶，   Tomorrow,

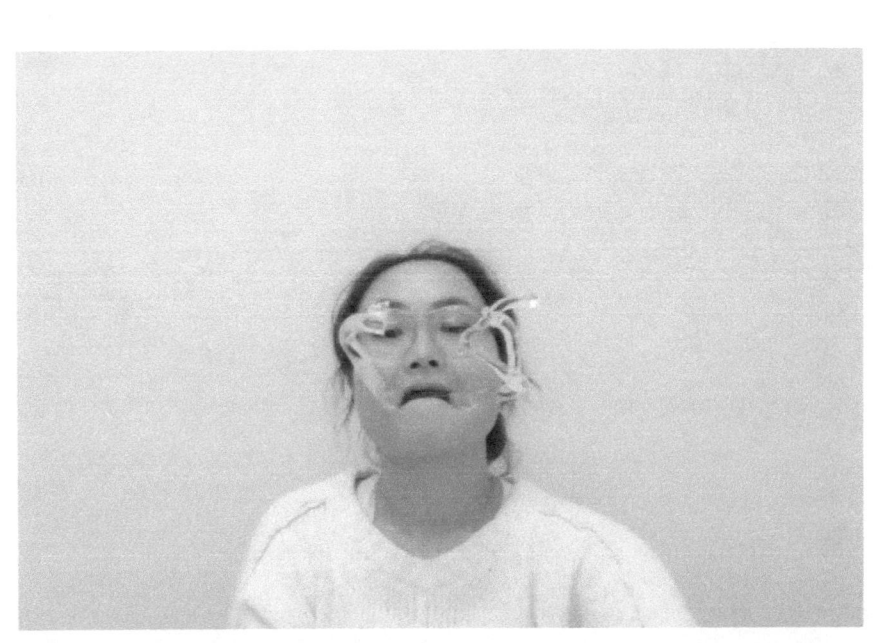

that

他们用

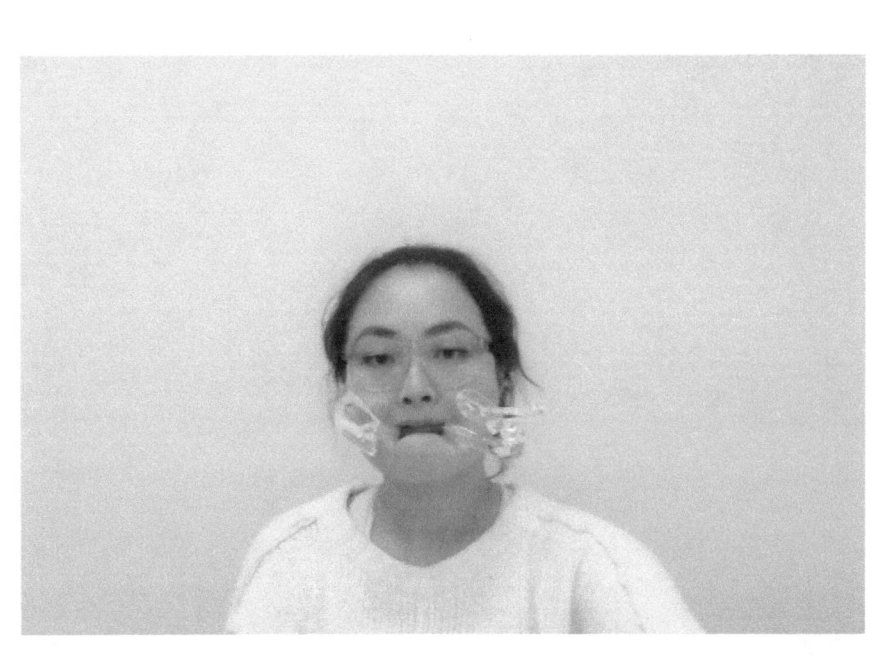

芝村明阳

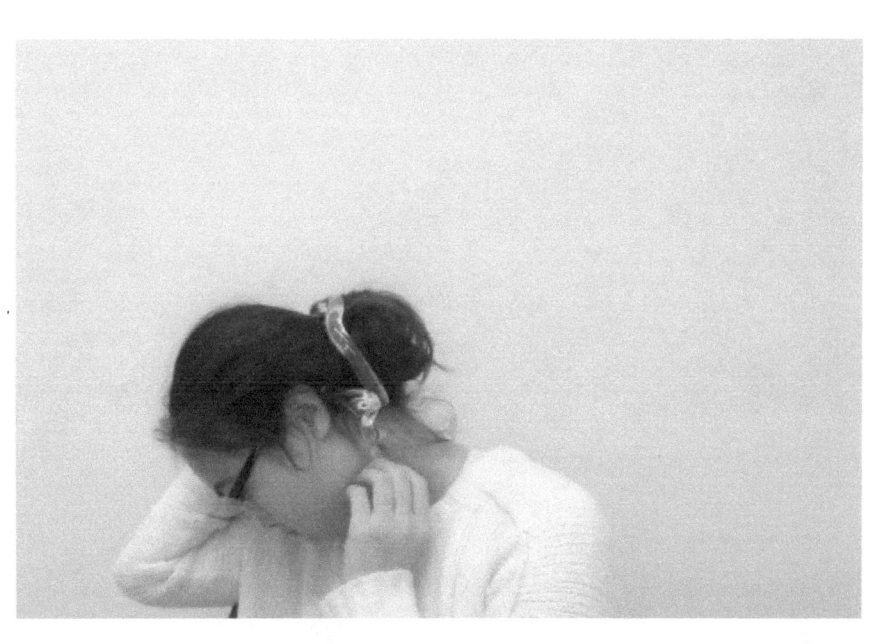

下呈

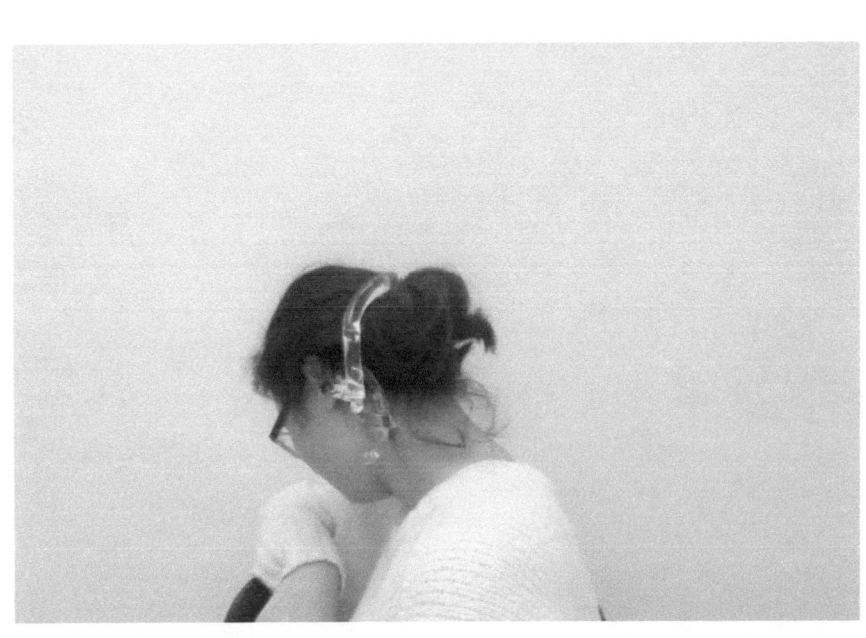

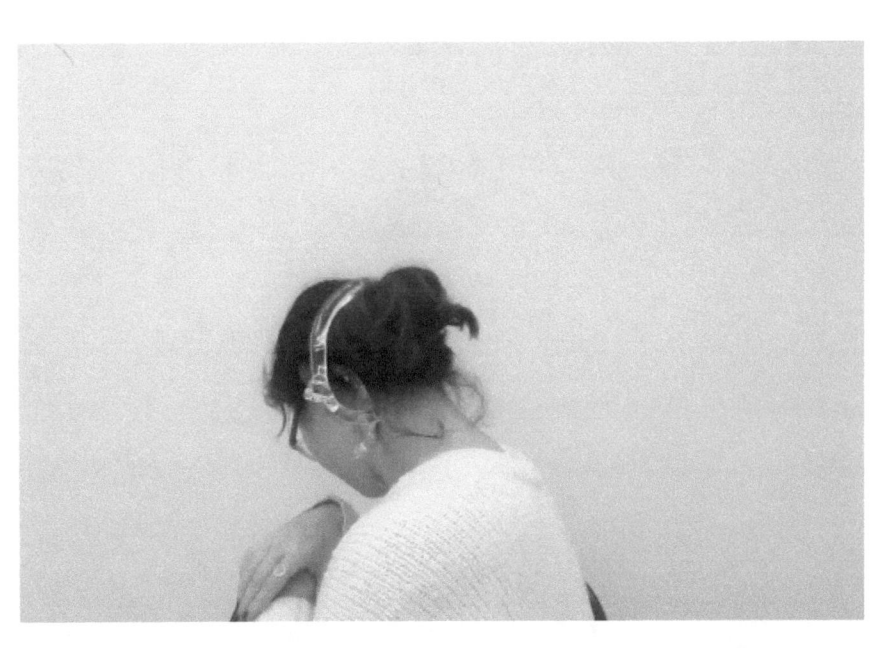

味道，   tell

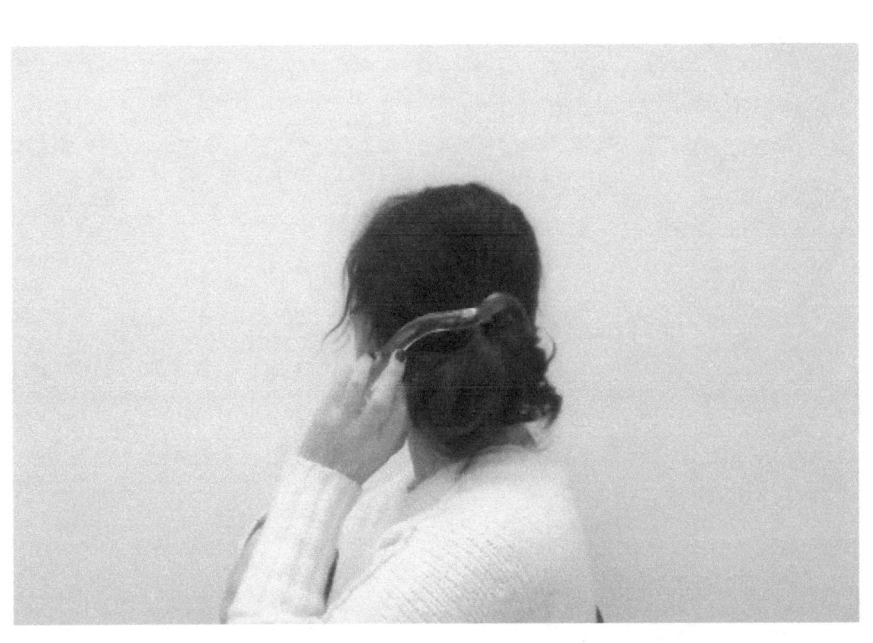

(teach)

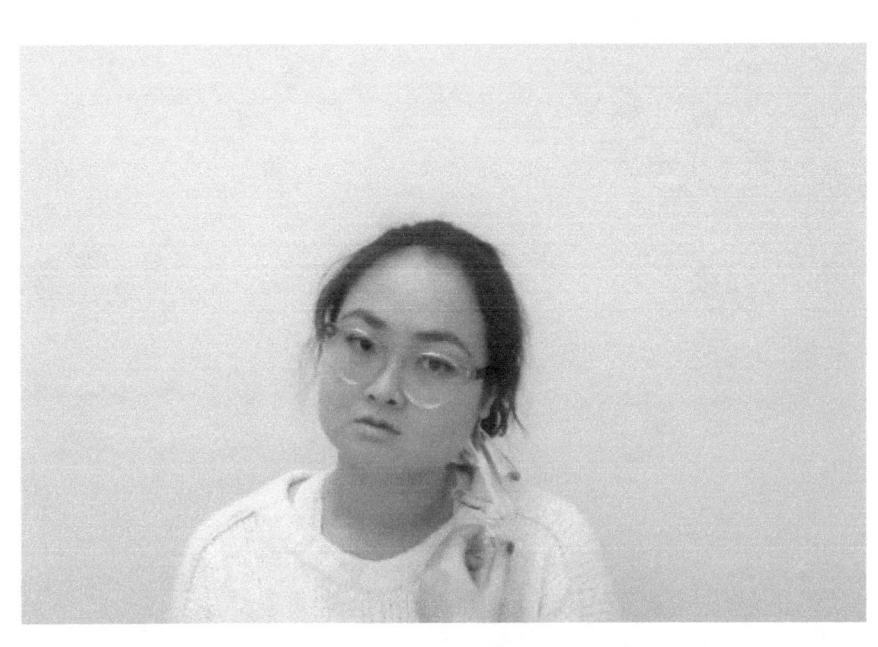

常识。

through

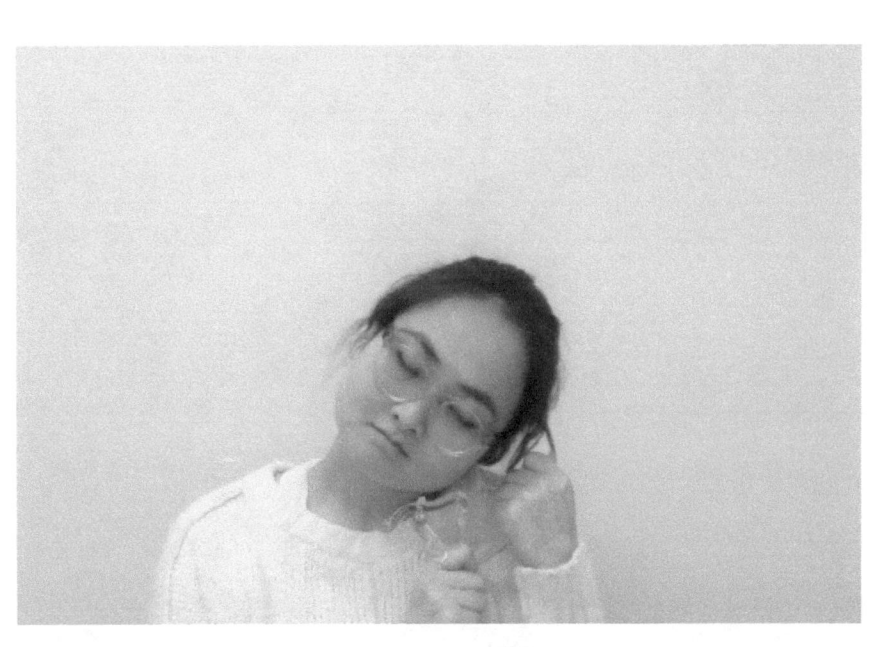

tongues.

洋涇浜

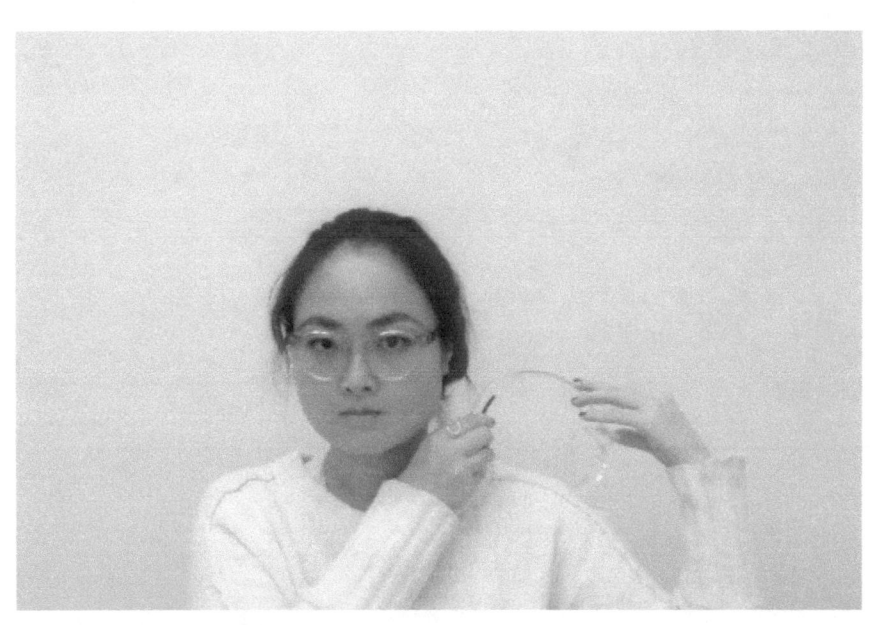

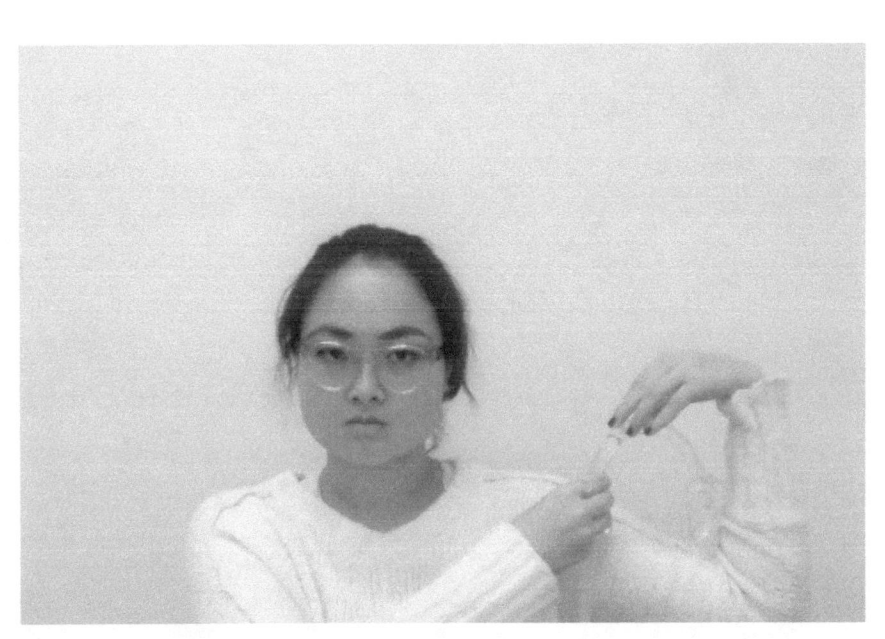

潜水

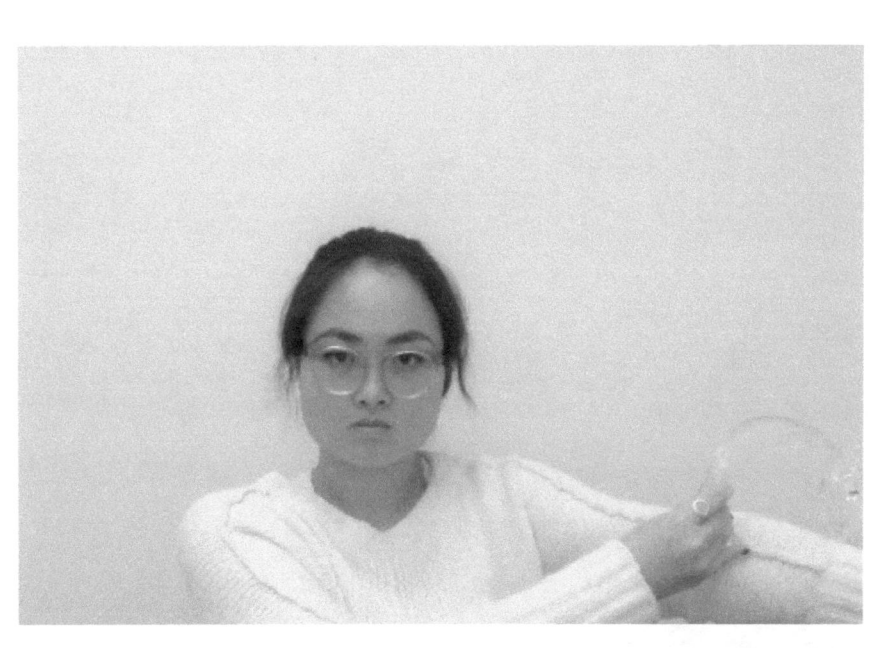

的

tongues.

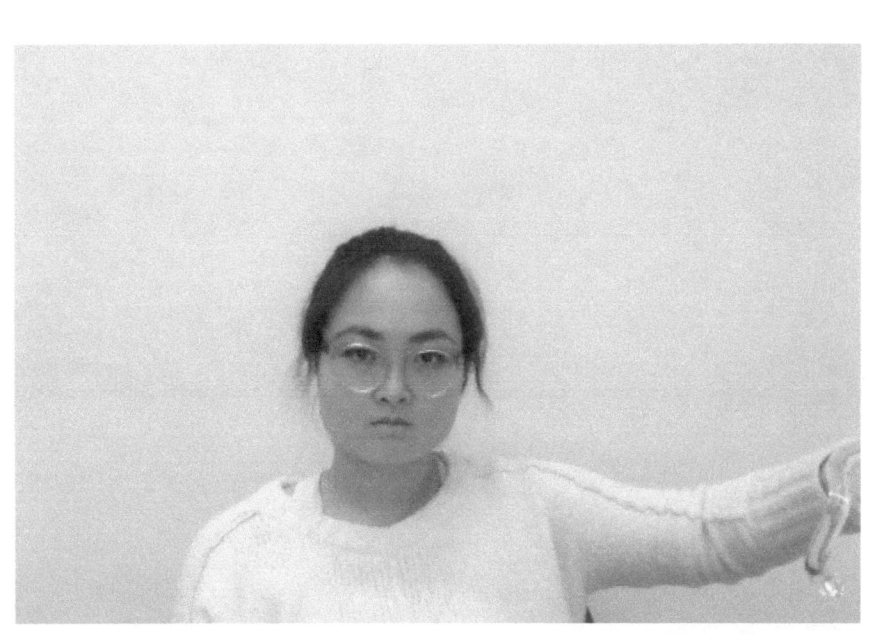

Temporal,

地粹。

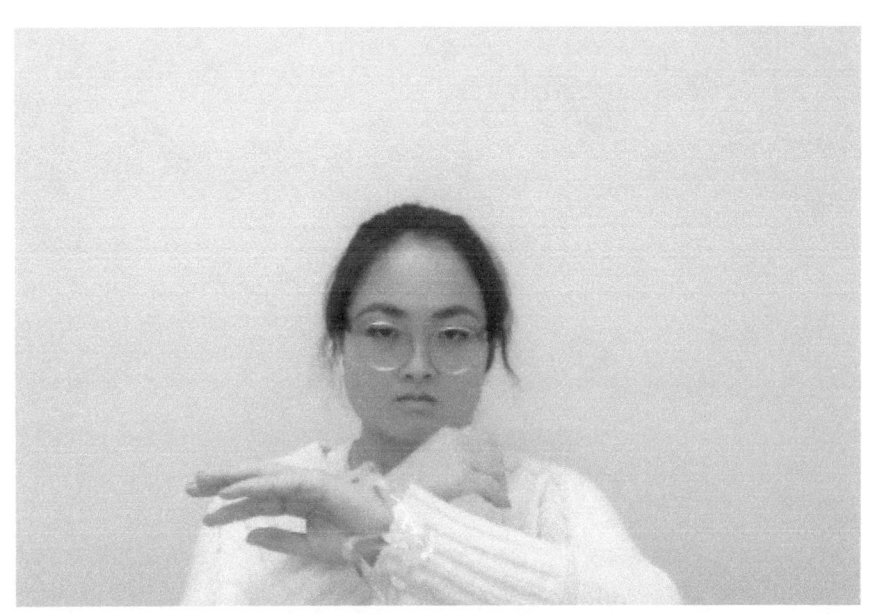

temporal

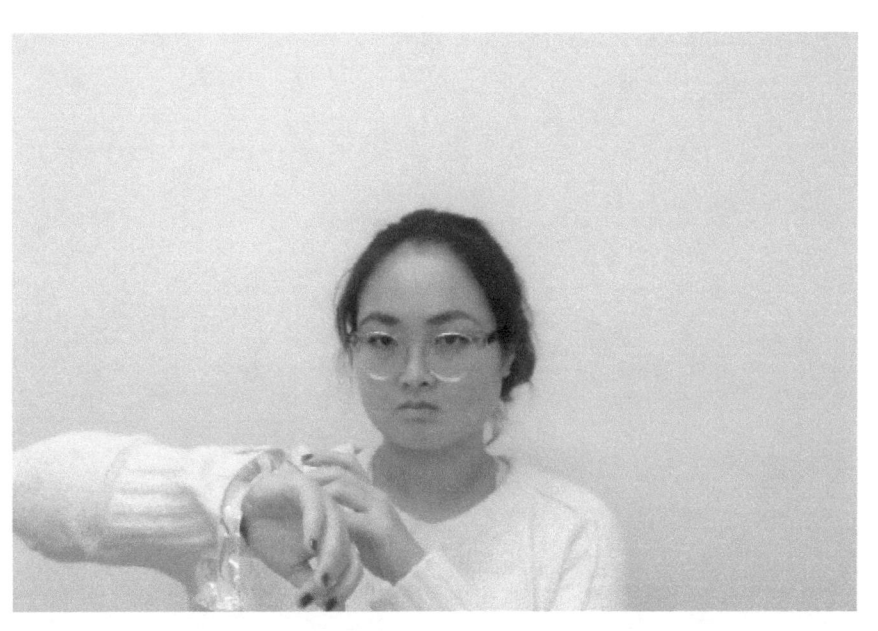

的 terrain.

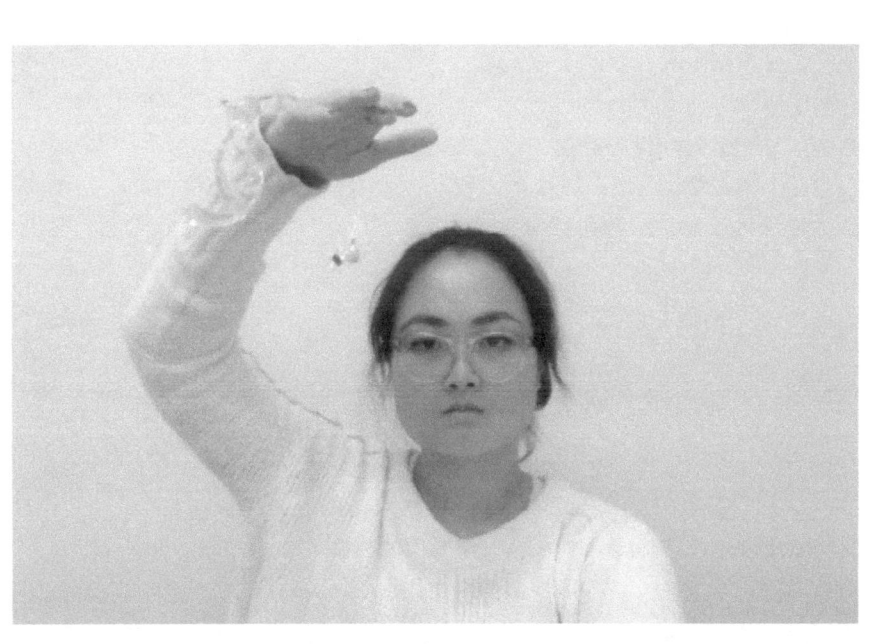

Trembling,

紆干。

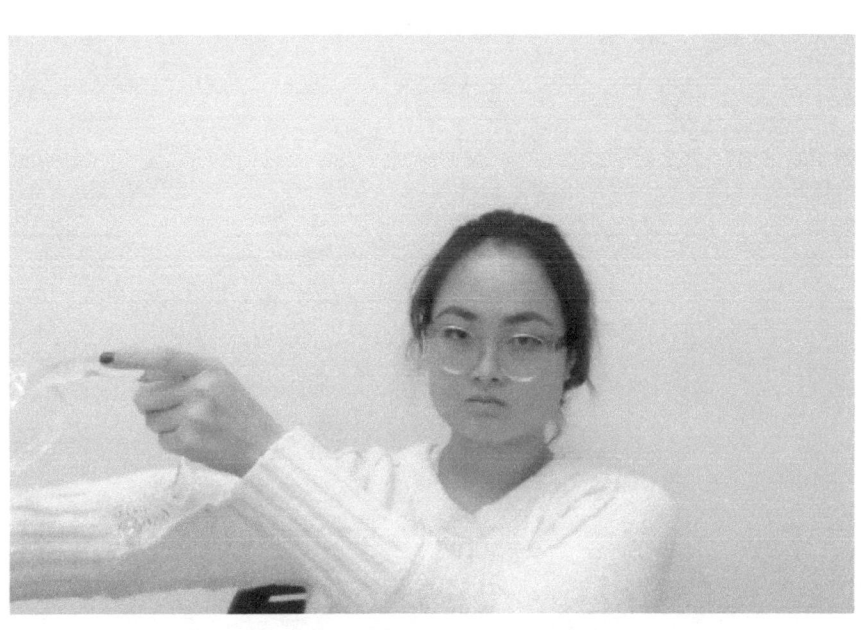

trembling

花枝

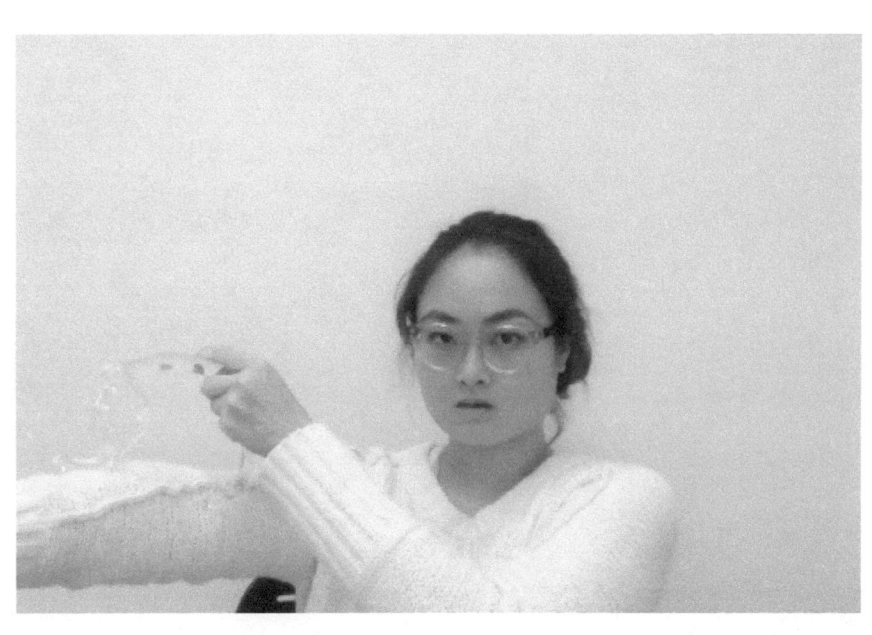

territory.

'山,

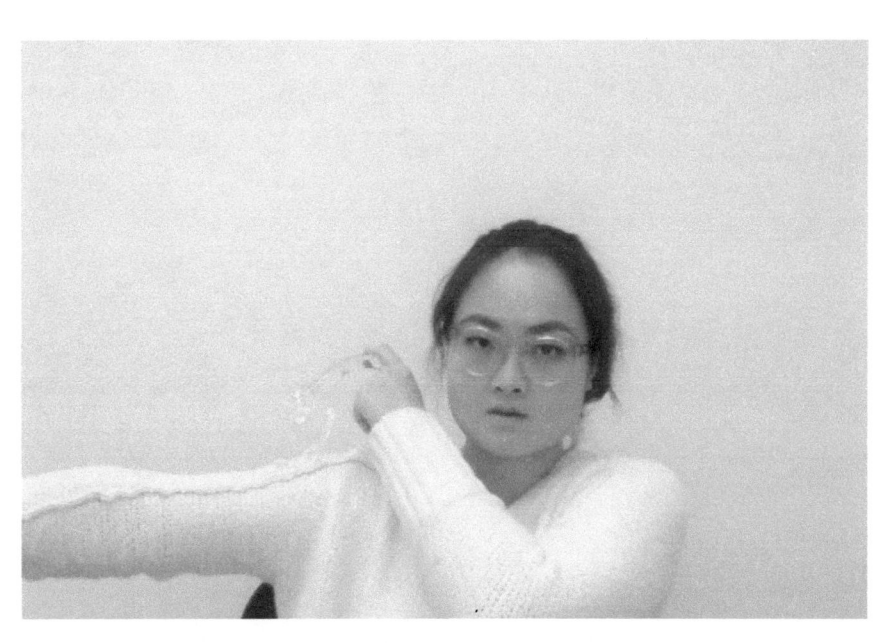

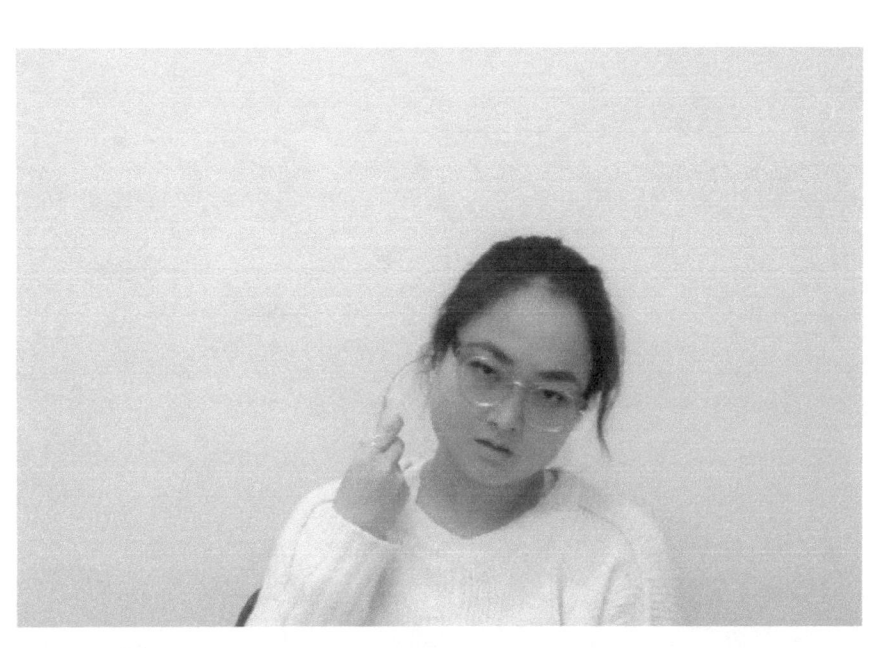

It,

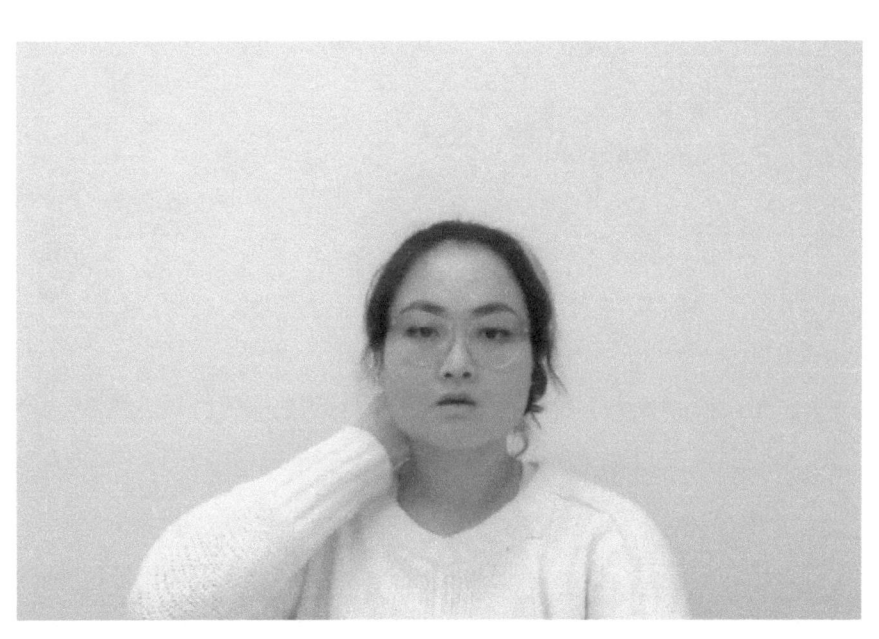

疲惫的玩具。   this

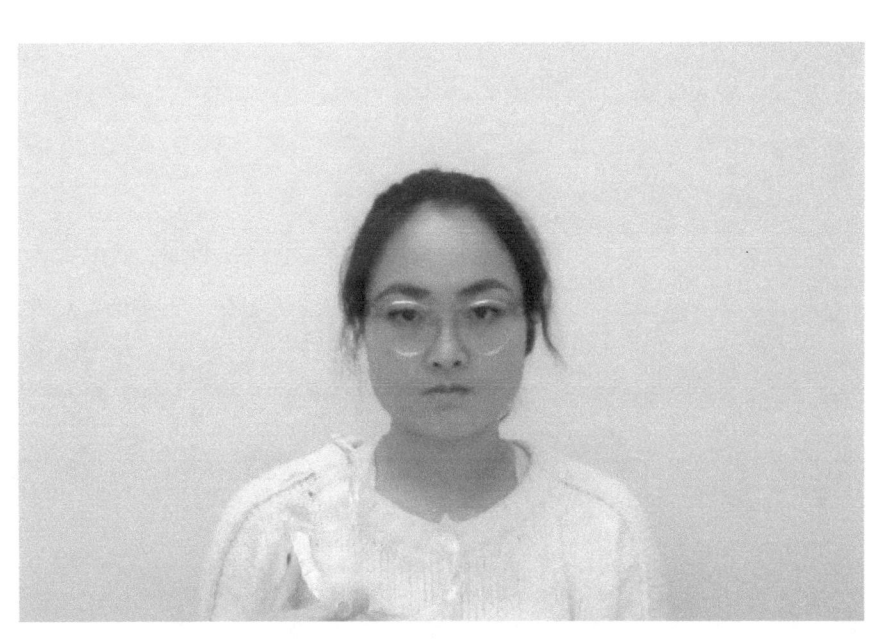

tired

卍

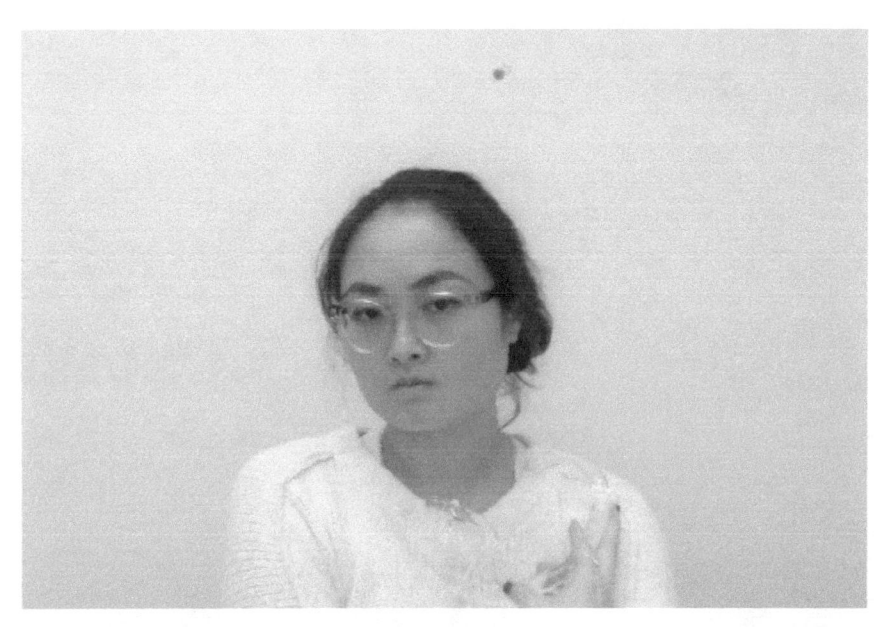

toy,

不得，

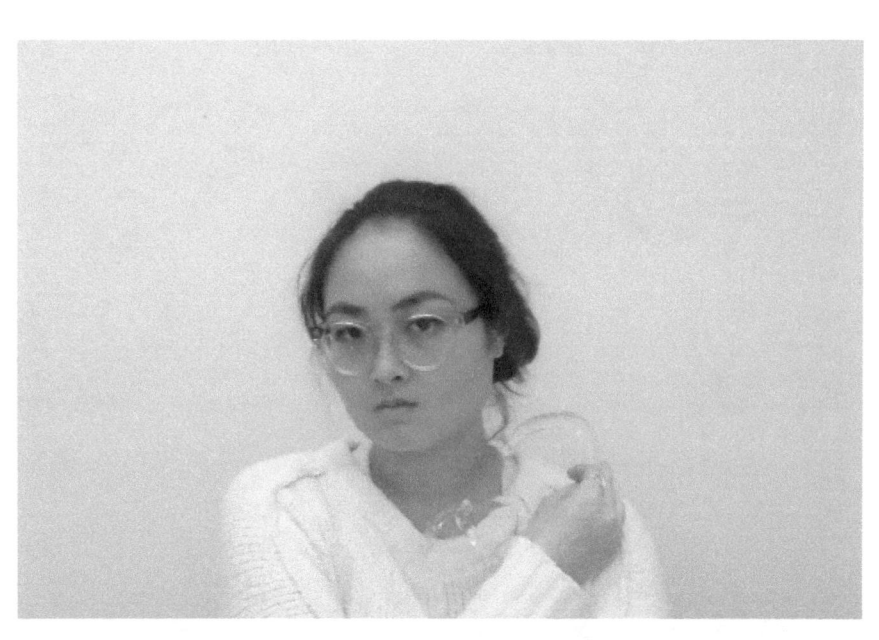

台北

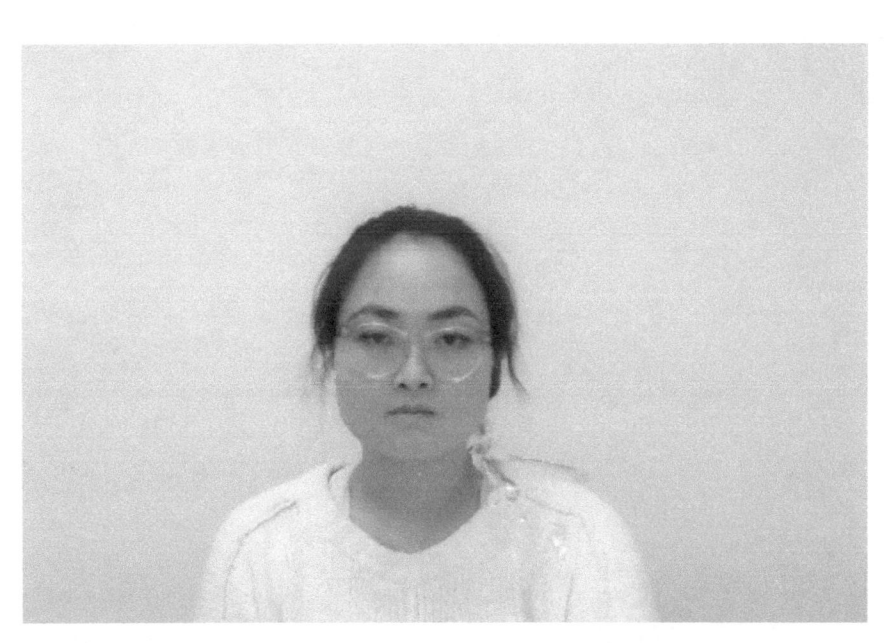

Thanks,

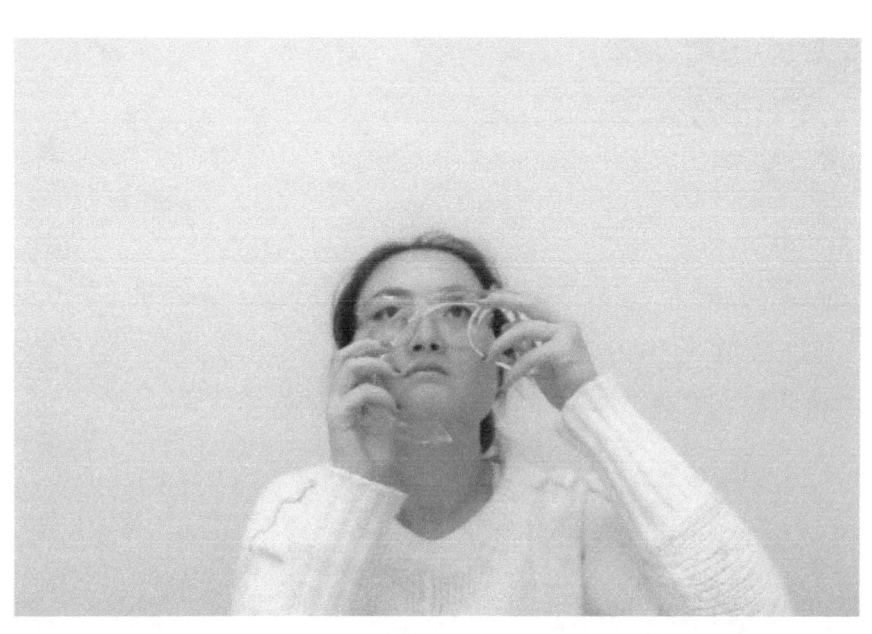

though.

慨。

It 09/28/15

09/28/15 它

交织。

Interweave.

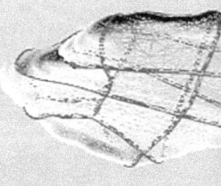

迸。

交织。

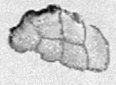

Interweave.

Rift.

瑰丽。

缝。

交织。

交织。

Interweave.

Rift.

Estrange.

疏离。

缝。

交织。

Interweave.

Rift.

Estrange.

Pope Francis came. The moon was absent.

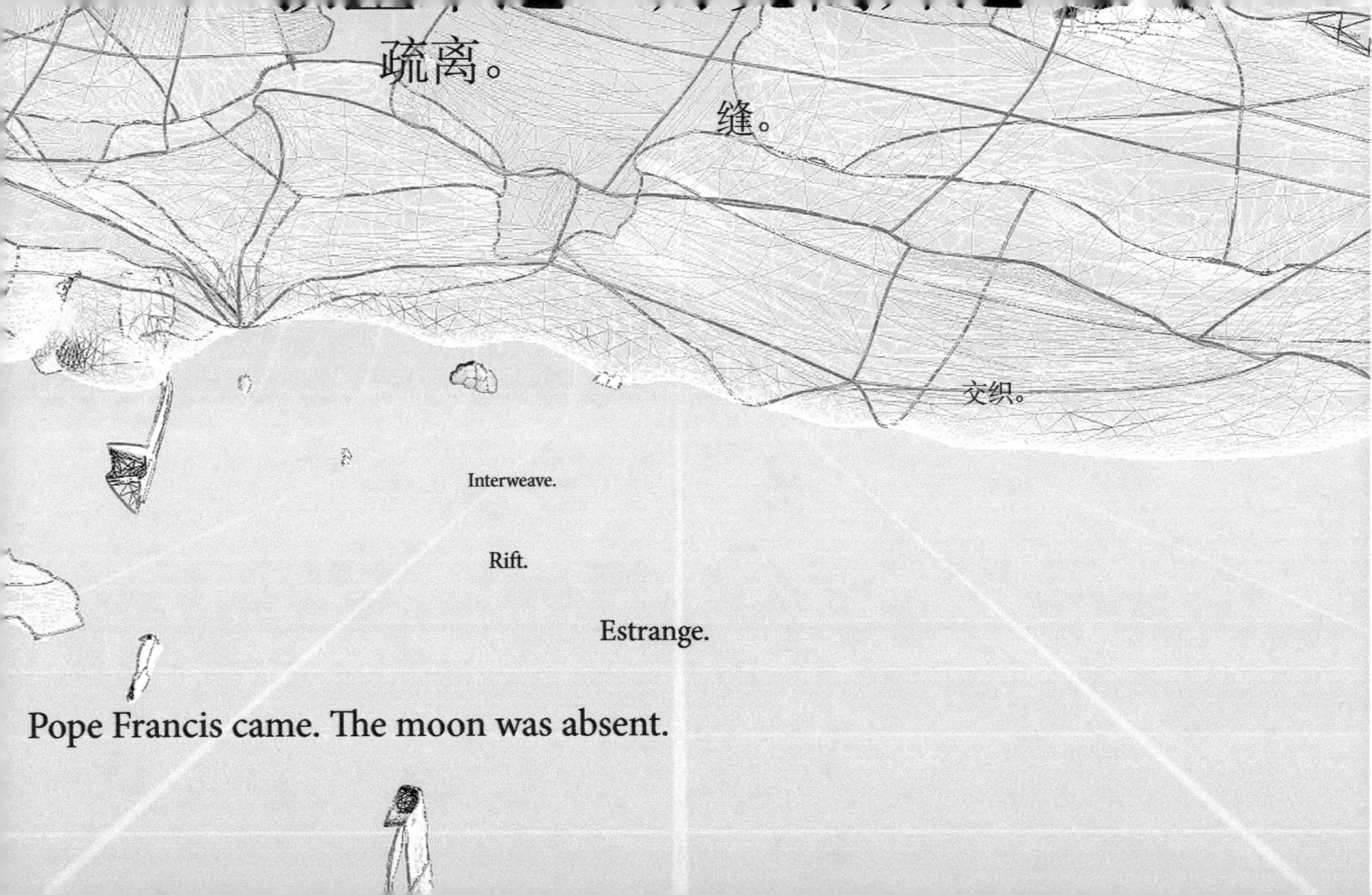

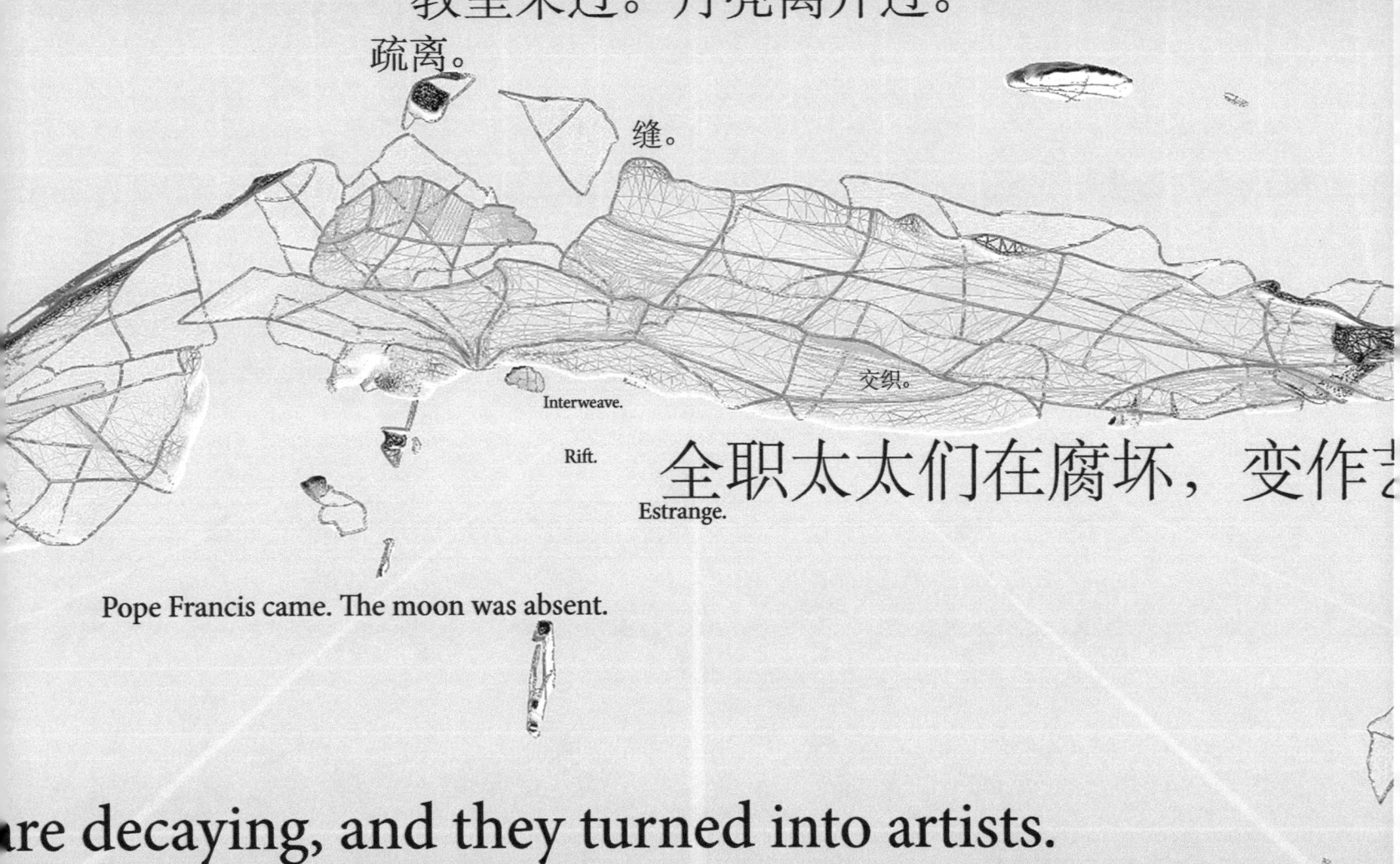

敎皇來過。 月亮離開過。

疏離。

縫。

交织。

Interweave.

Rift.

全职太太们在腐坏，变作艺

Estrange.

Pope Francis came. The moon was absent.

re decaying, and they turned into artists.

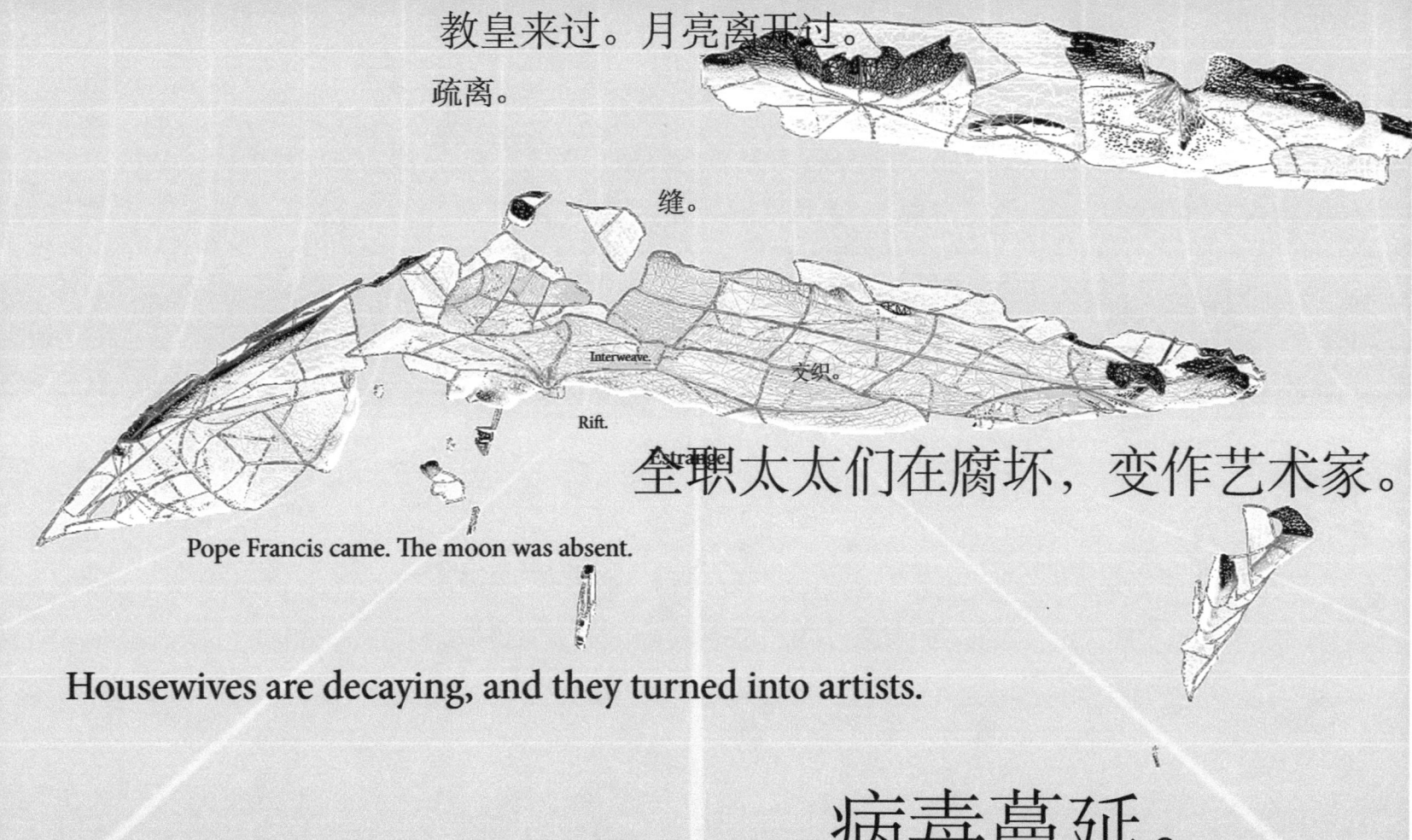

教皇来过。月亮离开过。

疏离。

缝。

Interweave.

文织。

Rift.

Estrange.

全职太太们在腐坏，变作艺术家。

Pope Francis came. The moon was absent.

Housewives are decaying, and they turned into artists.

病毒蔓延。

Epidemics.

教皇来过。月亮离开过。

疏离。

缝。

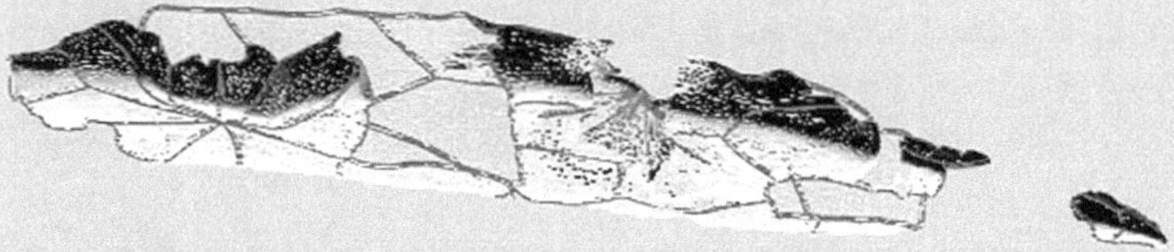

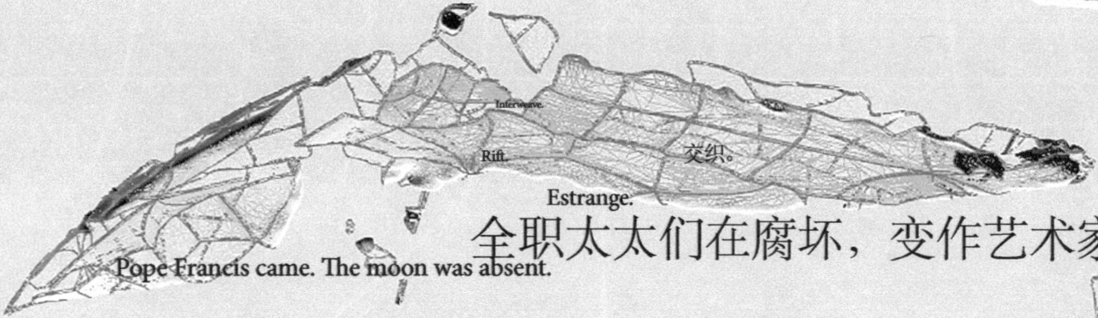

Interweave.

Rift.　　突织。

Estrange.

全职太太们在腐坏，变作艺术家。

Pope Francis came. The moon was absent.

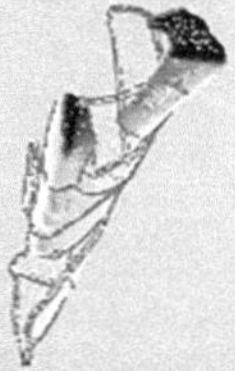

Housewives are decaying, and they turned into artists.

病毒蔓延。

人类的大灾难。

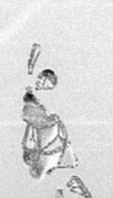

教皇来过。月亮离开过。

疏离。

Epidemics.

缝。

在它里面。

交织。

Rift.

全职太太们在腐坏，变作艺术家。

Estrange

Pope Francis came. The moon was absent.

Housewives are decaying, and they turned into artists.

病毒蔓延。

人类的大灾难。

In it.

它 09/29/15

小小的它，看起来小小的，但别小看它。
它是一个纪念品，不是什么新花样。
作为一个纪念品，它来自未能确定的场景，和那个谁，为
了什么，在一个普通的日子。

°日朱晋业荓

"节日快乐"到底是什么意思？所有的节日都必须要快乐
吗？快乐又算什么呢？哈，好便宜！离开原型的复制啊，
再复制。
在这个虚拟的世界里（正如鲍德里亚预言的那样），这个
小小的它和小小的真。
谢谢啊，那么所有的节日你都要快乐，你要永远快乐。

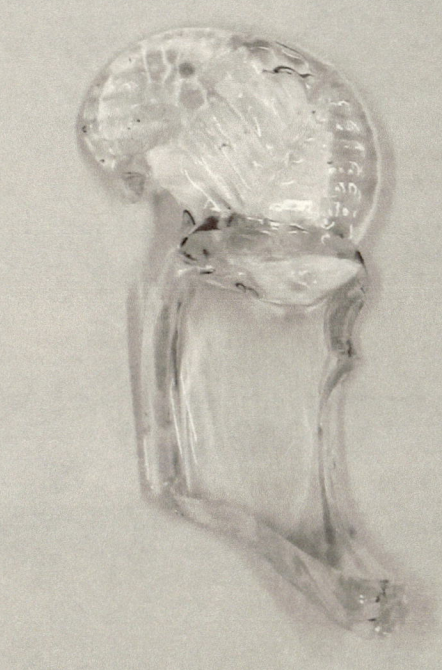

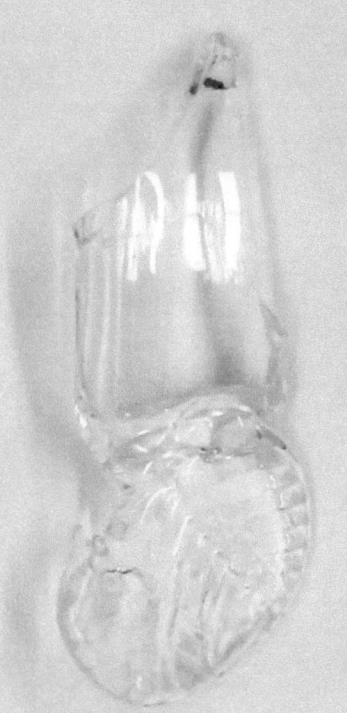

It 09/29/15

Little, little It, be little, yet don't belittle It.

It is not some sort of novelty, rather a souvenir. A souvenir from a precarious scene, with whomever, for whatever, in a normal day.

NOT IN A FESTIVAL.

"Happy Festival," doesn't make any sense. How much is happy? Hah, how cheap! A copy of a copy, without an original. In this virtual world as Jean Baudrillard predicted, the little It is little real.

Well, thank you, and I wish you a happy festival, any festival.

it हैं
10/
01/
15

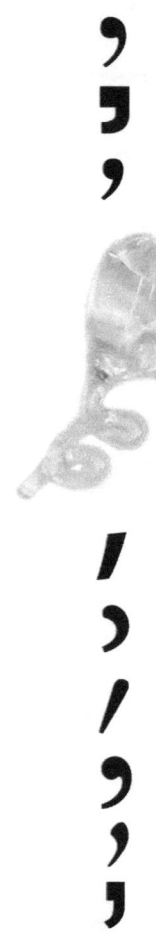

,

"在苍茫的大海上狂风卷集着乌云在乌云和大海之间"

"Over the gray plain of the sea the wind gathers storm clouds Between the clouds and the sea" (Maxim Gorky, The Song of Sea Swallow) sandwiched a comma

（---高尔基，[海燕]） It

夹	postponed
了	a
一	possibility
个	A
逗	cake-like
号	dinosaur
它	egg
延	is
期	endowed
了	encountered
一	enveloped
种	but
可	postponed
能	Slow-slow-motion
性	Gentle-gentle-men
一	completed
个	an
蛋	extinction
糕	of
样	this
貌	possibility
的	I'm
恐	gently
龙	offering

蛋被天生赋予偶然邂逅包围遮盖同时期延男人用放慢的速

a
comma
here
with
both
hands
to
cancel
an
event

度以及温柔的态度灭绝了这种可能性让我在这里用双手虔

诚地奉上一个逗号取消发生

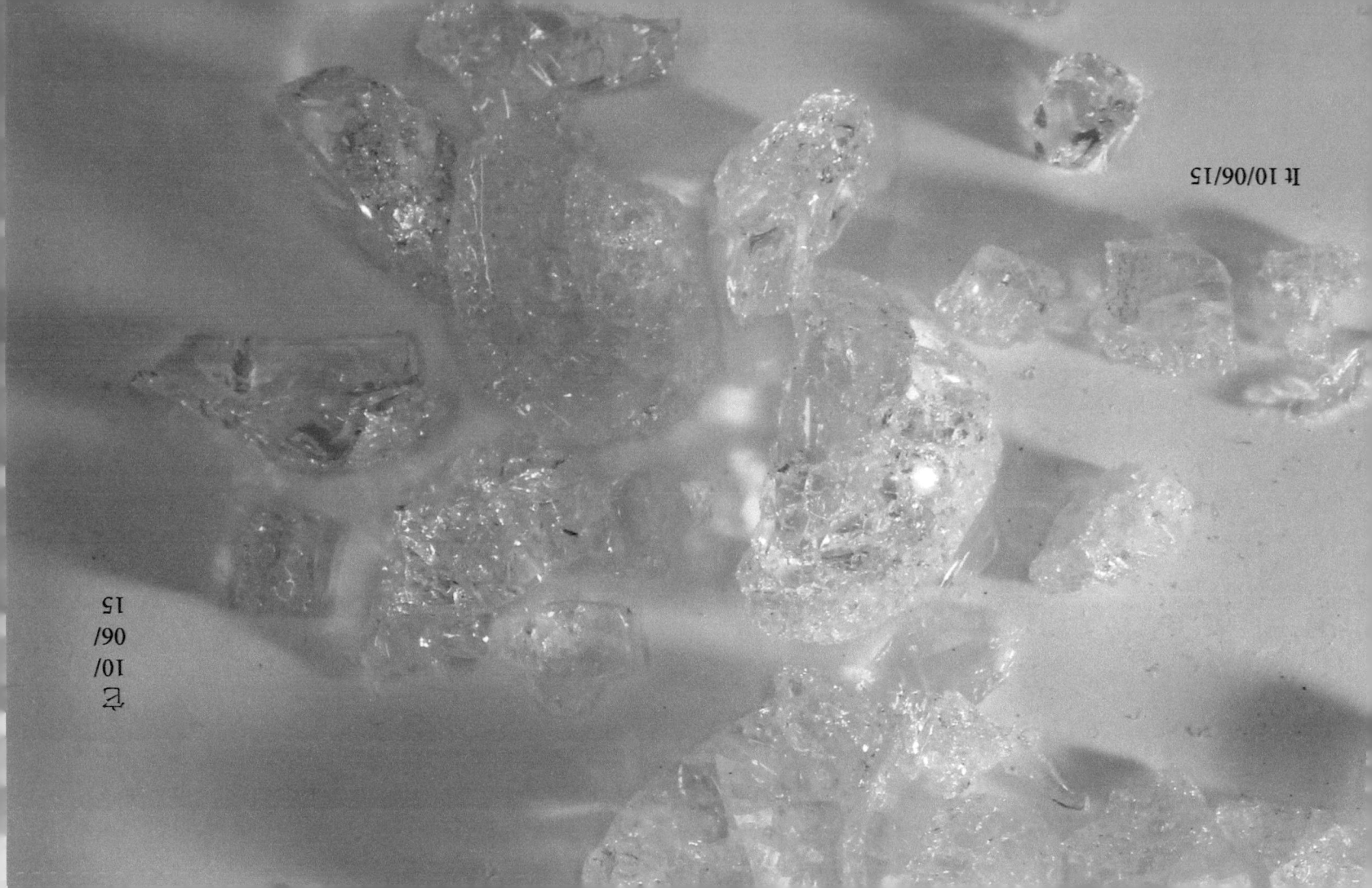

Some tragedies wouldn't be sad if people took pictures of them.

当人们给悲剧拍照时，他们似乎就不再令人哀愁。

“我当初就料到它会这样。”

它就是一个计划，你不应该难过。

它只是一个测试，一个实验，不是真的。

"Yeah, I knew it would happen."

It is a plan, so you shouldn't be upset about it.

It is just a testing, an experiment, not real.

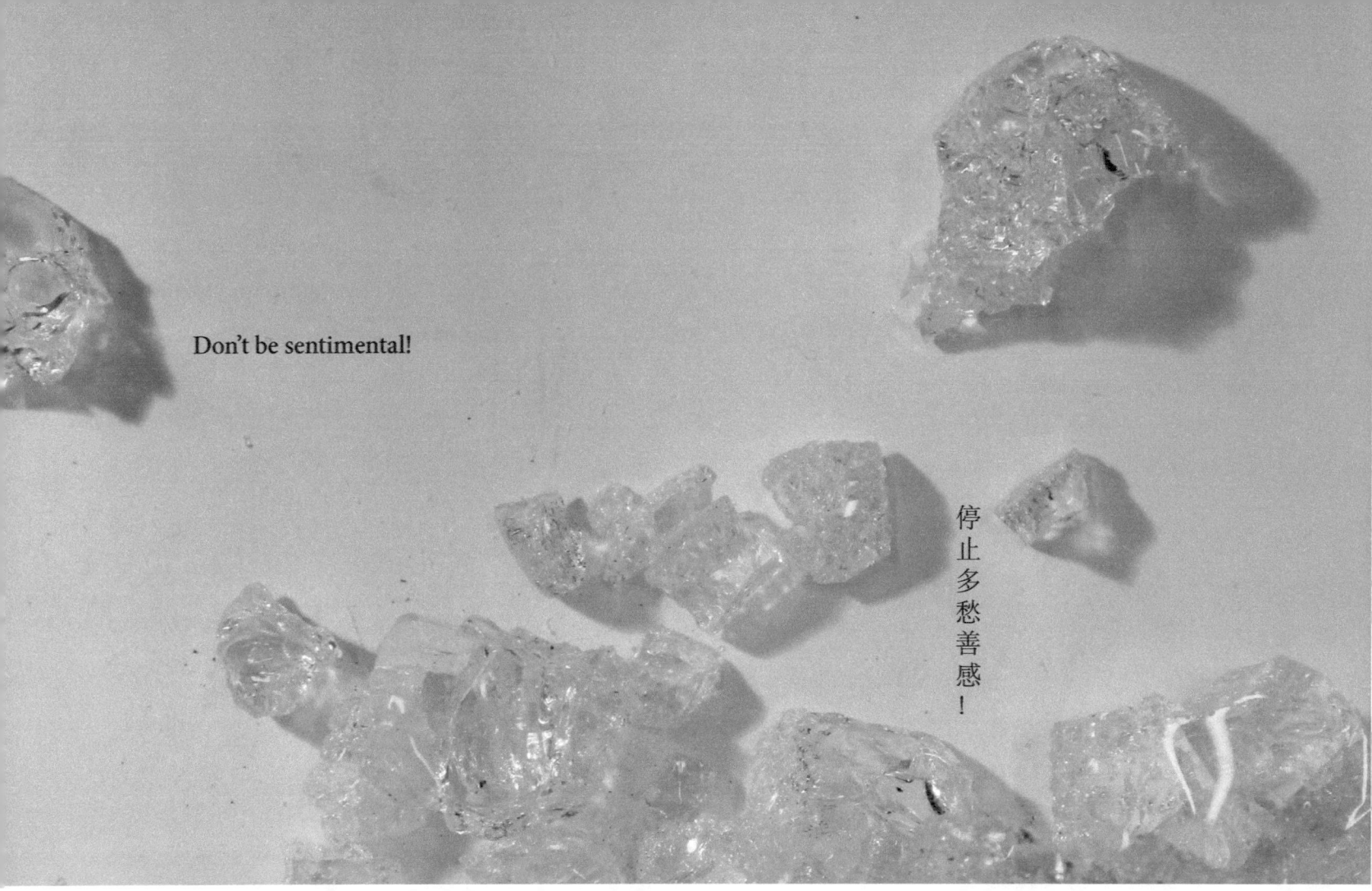

Don't be sentimental!

停止多愁善感！

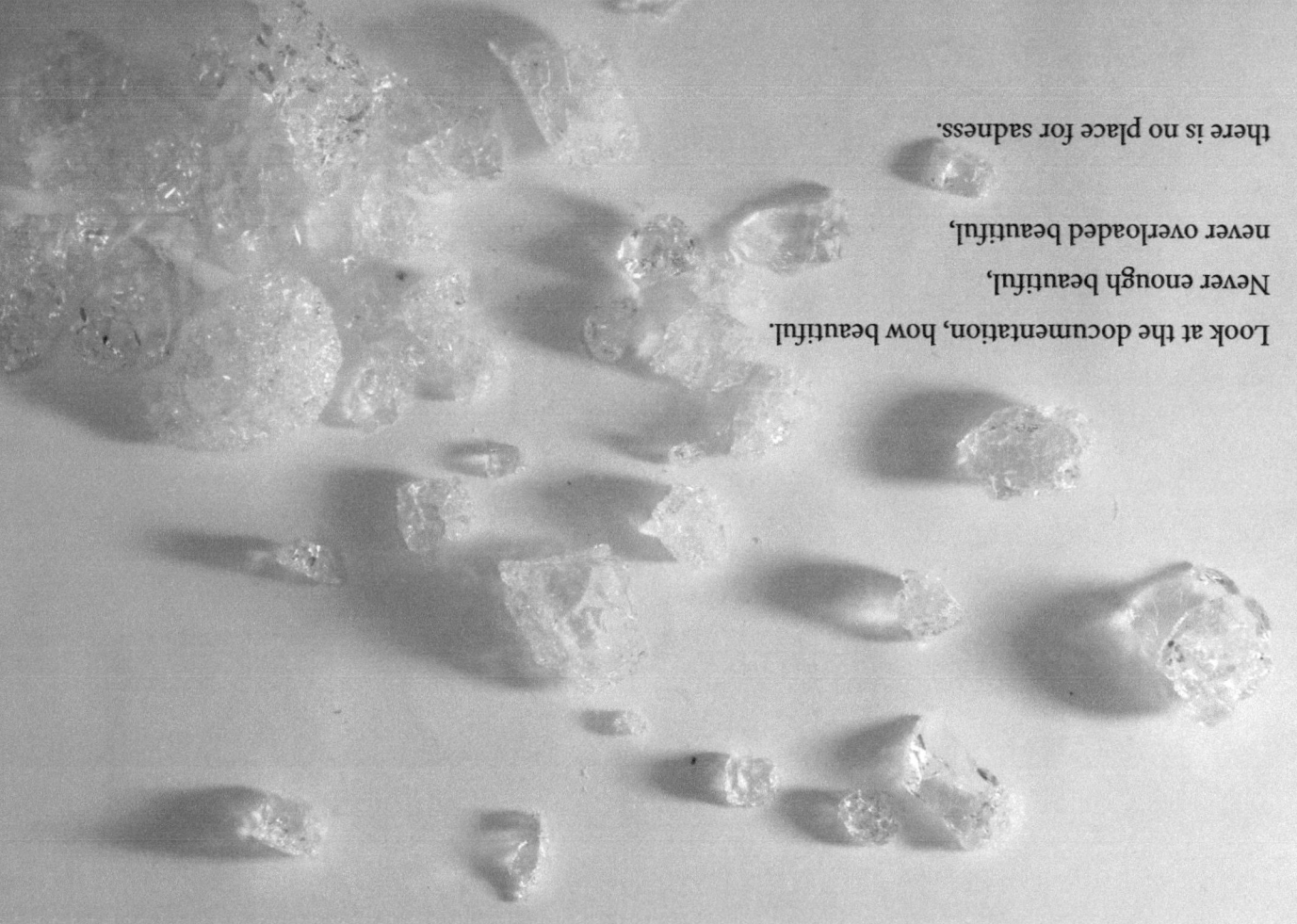

Look at the documentation, how beautiful.
Never enough beautiful,
never overloaded beautiful,
there is no place for sadness.

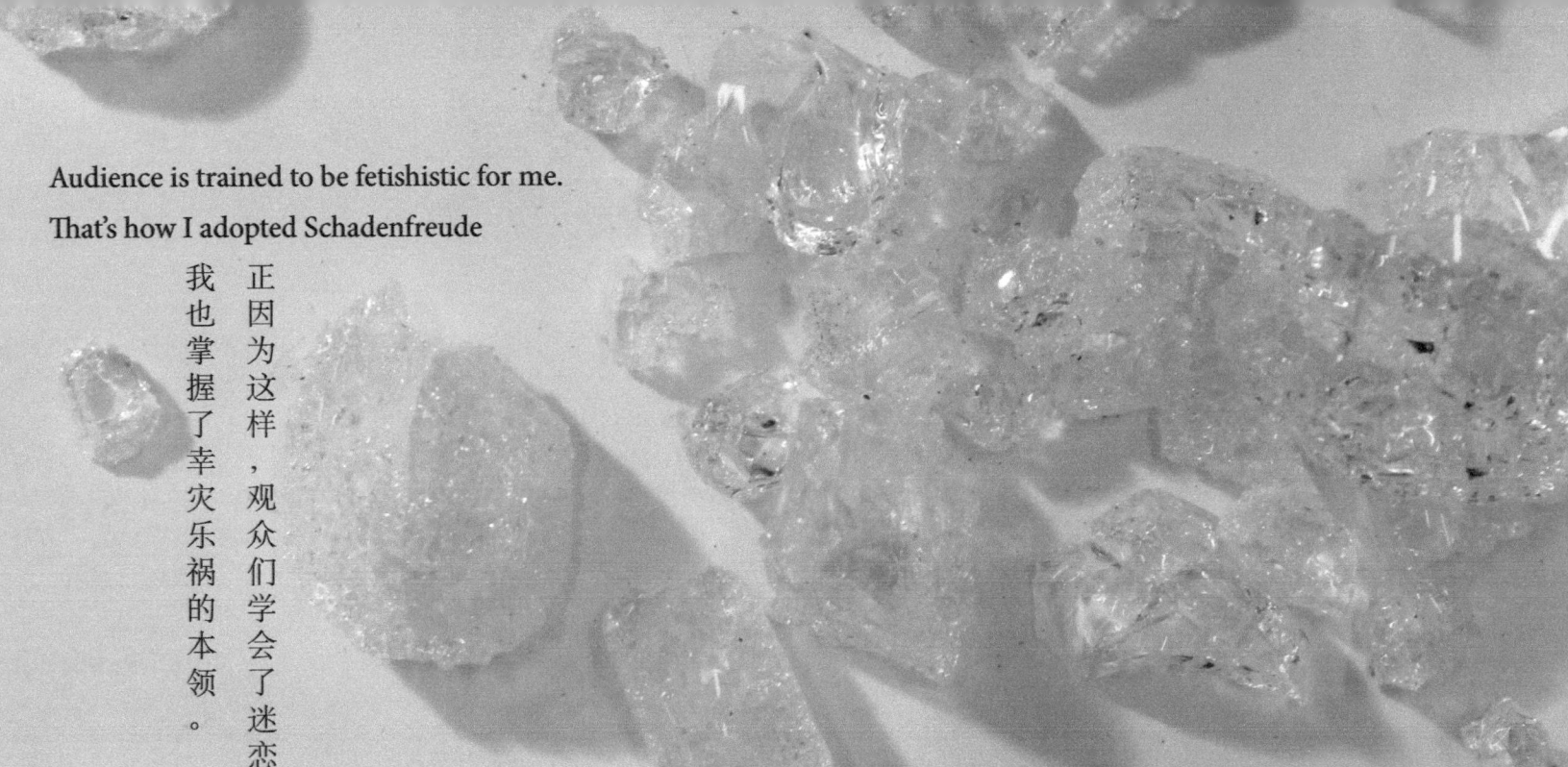

Audience is trained to be fetishistic for me.
That's how I adopted Schadenfreude

正因为这样，观众们学会了迷恋我的套路，我也掌握了幸灾乐祸的本领。

It 10/13/15

10/13/15 它

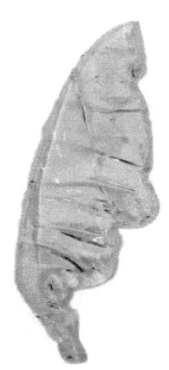

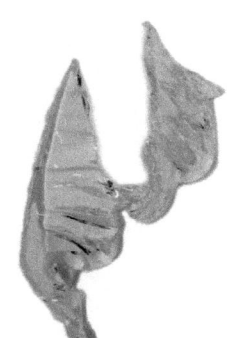

去 Divorce

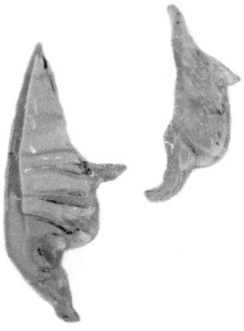

风
和

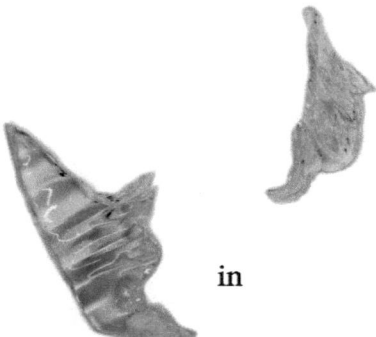

in

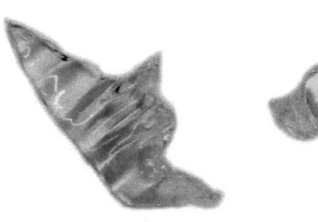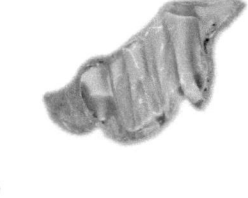

日
丽

a

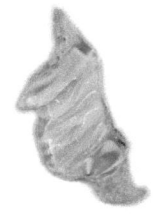

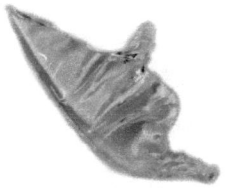

里 　 　 　 　 good

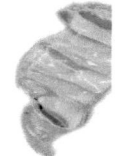

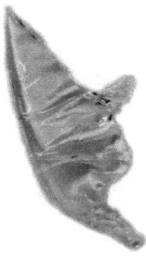

离婚

day

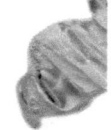

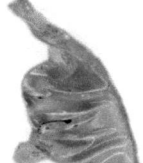

o   .

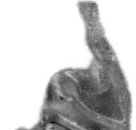

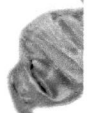

Mis 误 understanding 解
in 无 competent hostility 能力的仇视
clichés 陈词滥调们 may 也会 update 更新换代
men 人 will get old 老了 and leave 会死
读不懂 always 永远 have 有 more 好多 to understand
mean 同 while 时
new methodology 方法论也 is 永远 expected 期待着 to be 被 created 创造
the 繁花 randomness 和 of 世界 cosmos 的 and 无 flowers 序
chaos 乱

discover 探索 an 个 aspect 切面 —even by taking advantage of yourself 在这个过程中利用自己也是

好的 — 把 to 失落了 sort out 的 the lost 整理出来
赞 compliments 美 are cheap 其实特别轻
weight 无关 nothing 痛痒
去 join
联结 join together
there 会 will be light 有光